You Can Get There from Here

Books by Shirley MacLaine

"Don't Fall Off the Mountain"
You Can Get There from Here

You Can Get There from Here

Shirley MacLaine

W · W · NORTON & COMPANY · INC · New York

FIRST EDITION

Copyright © 1975 by Shirley MacLaine

ALL RIGHTS RESERVED
Published simultaneously in Canada
by George J. McLeod Limited, Toronto
PRINTED IN THE UNITED STATES OF AMERICA

Library of Congress Cataloging in Publication Data
MacLaine, Shirley, 1934–
    You can get there from here.
     1. MacLaine, Shirley, 1934–   I. Title.
PN2287.M18A34 1975   791.43'028'0924   74–23555
ISBN 0–393–07489–7

1 2 3 4 5 6 7 8 9 0

For Pete

You Can Get There from Here

One

LET ME START at the end: in Las Vegas. It was twenty after eight on July 12, 1974. I stood in the wings of the giant hotel theater set in the starkness of the American desert. I heard the roll of tympani, and then the strains of the theme from *The Apartment*. There were no more minutes left, either for delay or for thought or for hesitation. An oddly detached voice called my name. I walked out on the stage, and started to sing:

> *If they could see me now . . .*
> *That little gang of mine . . .*

A roar of applause came up as the spotlight hit me. I could feel the soft peach chiffon playing around my legs and see the zircons glittering on my shoulder straps. It was Las Vegas, a town that loved zircons because zircons had more class than rhinestones but lacked the permanence of diamonds.

> *. . . Eating fancy chow*
> *and drinking fancy wine.*

Gradually I began to recognize familiar faces at the long rows of tables topped with fancy chow and fancy wine, and as I kicked a leg high there was another roll of applause. The inside of my mouth was like cotton and my stomach lurched. Then quite suddenly, I was soaring, carried by the music, the words, the lights, and the velvet darkness of the vast room packed with that audience that

Oscar Hammerstein had once called "the big black giant." I spread my arms wide and felt joyous and exalted and free.

> *I'd like those stumblebums to see for a fact*
> *The kind of top-drawer, first-rate chums I attract*

Right in front of me were Carroll O'Connor and his wife, Nancy, and behind them, glowing like a golden presence, was Goldie Hawn. Off to my left was Gwen Verdon, red-haired and beautiful, dazzling me with her electric smile, and over to the right was Matty Troy, the Democratic boss of New York's Queens County. I could see Pat Cadell and Fred Dutton, with whom I had traveled through so many strange towns during the tragic McGovern campaign. In another part of the darkened theater were Sam Brown and Dave Mixner, the insistent young with whom I had marched on Washington to protest the killing in Asia. Lucille Ball sat in a back booth, she who had given me so much laughter and so much instruction; and beside her was Ginger Rogers, who had inspired me to want to dance when I was a little girl. There were dozens and dozens of others, friends from politics and publishing, from newspapers and magazines, from show business, from foreign countries. Top-drawer, first-rate friends. It was as if all the important phases of my life over the past ten years sat before me.

> *All I can say is wow!*
> *Just look at where I am!*
> *Tonight I landed, pow!*
> *Right in a pot of jam!*

I loved the way I felt; strong and resilient and sinuous, with plenty of breath to spare and easy, sharp movements to dance with. There had been a year of running on the beach, long hours spent in sweaty gymnasiums, early mornings in dance studios. I had given up bread, potatoes, Hershey bars with almonds, and homemade chocolate chip cookies—the mainstay of my diet along the campaign trail. No more cigarettes, no more sedentary hours writing a book. The dryness in my mouth vanished and I could feel adrenalin flooding my body. Back in the dressing room there were masses of flowers and hundreds of telegrams from well-wishers. While getting ready I thought about all the people I had met over the past few years and wondered what they were doing this evening: the people I had worked with on my disastrous TV series, all the people of America I had talked with during the campaign, the people I had greeted in strange dusty towns in China. Absurdly, given the setting, I thought of Chou En-lai, who had suffered a heart attack, and pictured his wife, Teng Ying-ch'ao, sitting through the nights with him. I wondered whether either of them could ever understand that my being here, on this huge stage in super-capitalistic Las Vegas, had everything to do with them, and all their comrades.

> *What a set-up! Holy cow.*
> *They'd never believe it . . .*

The dancers were on the stage now. Together we kicked our legs high in the air, kicking for laughter and joy, kicking because we loved to make people feel good, kicking because we loved to feel good ourselves. The audience began to applaud again and we kicked higher. I moved to stage left and suddenly saw Margaret Whitman, silver-haired and dignified, who had been with me in China. I remembered what she had said to a friend that afternoon. "China makes you feel anything is possible. That's why Shirley's here." I had thought about that all day, turning it over in my mind.

With my straw hat raised in the air, I finished the opening number. The final applause was explosive, led by Dan Melnick, the head of MGM, which was no longer a major studio but which ran the hotel in which I was appearing, and I remembered an afternoon a few years before when everything had seemed bleak and forlorn. It was a time when I, like almost everyone I knew, had stopped laughing. Now Dan, sitting next to Kirk Kerkorian, who now owned the company that owned Metro, was laughing. So was every other person in the room. And for some reason, I felt as if I had just begun to live my life again. After a long time away I was back doing what I had been trained to do in the first place. Only now I knew a lot more about who I was because the road back hadn't been an easy one.

Two

It was April of 1970, and I was standing in the middle of an empty street at the Metro-Goldwyn-Mayer studios in Culver City, on a day choked with smog. The walls of the sound stages climbed like the Kremlin around me. I walked toward the long flat building that housed the dressing rooms for stars, tried the front door, and found that it was locked. I peered through one of the streaked windows and there it was—my old dressing room. I had made four films and spent nearly two years of my life in that dressing room. The cream-colored woven curtains were still hanging and I could see the erratic old shower that never seemed to have hot water when we needed it at the end of a long day in body make-up. The record player table was in the same place—covered with dust. And I remembered how Frank Sinatra and Dean Martin once brought me a plate piled with Italian salami and then, smiling broadly, whipped out a dozen cannolis wrapped in waxed paper and plopped them on top of "Come Fly with Me."

I looked over the chintz-covered furniture and remembered how the sofa felt from that dressing room, deep and plush and permanent. At Metro, I had made the picture that changed my life, *Some Came Running*, and used that couch to rest between shots. That was the film in which I realized that I could make people laugh and cry at the same time. From that room I had adjusted to the feelings of what it meant to be a star. And yet from that same room, for a long time, I had trudged at the end of every day longing to do something more than just act.

I walked across the alleyway to Make-Up and Hairdressing. The door was open.

"Hello, can I come in?" I called. "Is anyone here?"

There was no answer. The sound of a forced air blower circulated through the hall. I walked in. A high-speed hair dryer stood alone and discarded. I walked slowly down the hallway and into the silent make-up rooms. Make-up lights surrounding the mirrors had been unscrewed and removed. More hair dryers stood arbitrarily discarded in the center of the rooms. Leather make-up chairs were askew and dusty and seemed to be begging to be correctly placed before their mirrors.

The forced air blower moaned from the Hairdressing Department down the hall and reminded me of a lonely wind I had heard once through a ghost town in gold rush country.

It almost seemed to beckon me, so I walked in. Ornate brass-bound work lights stared down at empty work tables beneath them. Two wooden wig blocks, studded with pins, tipped out from the work table into the air. In the corner the familiar icebox stood forlornly with its doors open. Rings of rust on the bottom shelf were the only testament that champagne once stood there chilling, waiting for celebration. This was the room where it all happened. The room that was more full of magic from six to nine every weekday morning than the dressing room of the Wizard of Oz himself. In those days, Metro-Goldwyn-Mayer was the studio where the action was and Make-Up and Hairdressing were where the stars got ready for it.

Across the threshold of the Metro gate would glide the biggest and most famous movie stars in the world, and for a long time in those years I was one of them. Sometimes we'd emerge from long black limousines and sometimes we drove ourselves. We'd saunter and slink into Make-Up and Hairdressing looking almost like regular people; except that we were supposed to be magical even when dressed in blue jeans, or slacks, even when our eyes were clogged with sleep and our minds filled with remnants of the night before.

The smell of freshly brewed coffee would greet us as we entered, promising that maybe the early morning wouldn't be so bad after all. Dean Martin swung an imaginary golf club while he sipped his coffee. Kirk Douglas's eyes constantly circulated, as though clocking all future phone numbers, and Robert Cummings would hand the make-up man a map of his face to be filled in with a 4-N pan stick to the letter of his instructions. The men stars joked and kidded with their make-up men, as if the joking and kidding would conceal the fact that they had deep-rooted vanities and often felt silly that someone else knew it.

We women stars cautiously circled the tray of freshly cut danish, holding back with iron discipline, and rarely having sugar or cream in our coffee. I wondered whether the others ate breakfast before they left their homes, and whether they had as much trouble getting up in the morning as I did. And somehow, whenever we stars discussed our personal habits we could never be sure what was true. We treated such things so casually and yet looked so controlled that one always sensed what *wasn't* said was more important than what was.

Women stars always were made up in the privacy of

isolated make-up rooms, so that only we and our make-up man knew "if we did or we didn't." Most of us did.

But when we came together in Sydney Guillaroff's Hairdressing Department, it was a magical transformation of crowned glories.

On a given day, lined up on the leather chairs, coffee cups steaming in front of us, you could find all of the stars of Metro. Greer Garson, swathed in a turquoise blue robe that set off her carrot-colored hair, would go directly to Wardrobe to be wrapped in white ermine for a fitting for the Academy Awards. Next to her Jean Simmons, recently divorced, would chat about the desirability of marriage. Deborah Kerr, thin-hipped and more bawdy than the world ever knew, would dispense a few well-known adjectives on the same subject while Sydney Guillaroff would refill her coffee cup and touch her shoulder in reassurance. Sydney was tall and graceful, and always wore finely sewn skintight linen shirts. He smoked tapered cigarettes which he lit with a flourish and seldom missed the unlit cigarette of a star two tables away. Sydney lived in a mansion, complete with gold faucets on his sinks and bathtubs, and gave parties to which one always wore black tie. Sydney wasn't truly interested in women who hadn't the potential for some sort of greatness. When he found one, he was available whenever necessary, enhancing the creativity of that woman and respecting even the smallest confidence. He knew more about the great women stars of Hollywood than their psychiatrists did.

Audrey Hepburn, all Dresden, would rise slowly with her small poodle and proceed to the sound stage as if on satin roller skates.

Debbie Reynolds, the pride of Burbank, bubbled into the room punching jokes and being cuddly.

Then came Elizabeth Taylor, chunky and looking twelve years younger with no make-up; she'd flop into any chair that was vacant, eating a cheese danish and plopping her feet up on the table in front of her. They were pudgy feet and I would tease her about them, saying that they looked like they should belong to a weightlifter. Sydney would light her cigarette and she would draw the smoke long and deep into her lungs with the same low-down basic oral gratification she lavished on the cheese danish. Then Sydney Guillaroff would go down the line as though painting and sculpting the beautiful hairstyles until we were prepared to face the cameras.

There was a camaraderie of shared purpose and shared fear in the Hairdressing Department at Metro. Everyone seemed to understand that our purpose was to go on those screens and be loved by strangers, but our fears were that it might not happen.

What a time it was in Hollywood then. It all seemed so natural and permanent; we never dreamed then that it was doomed. It flowed along like water finding its own level. Pictures were made because picture making was a way of life, and stars and talent and new ideas would simply sweep on with the creative currents.

It somehow never occurred to me, or anyone else I knew, that one day soon it all might be over.

We reveled in each other's company at "Hollywood Parties," frolicked in the surf at Malibu, tooled down to Palm Springs on the weekends, and went in groups to Las Vegas when the Clan played the big rooms.

Somehow *we* felt real and the *outside* world didn't. Our homes were luxurious salons, but if you tried to turn the talk to anything serious, you were viewed as a wet blanket. We *knew* there was trouble somewhere out there; we just didn't want it to infect what we believed was our "creativity," or dampen spirits which were "required" to remain positive. So the jokes and laughter rolled on. Even when someone became involved in a "cause" it was because a big political name had asked her or him to. Fun and lushness were the things of life if you belonged to the upper regions of the Hollywood Haven. You did two or three pictures a year, limited your friends to the people you worked with, hired a firm of lawyers and C.P.A.'s to save you taxes, paid an agent and a publicity man, and looked around for reasons to continue doing more of the same.

I fled Hollywood many times because I had to. It was like eating too much rich food. But I always loved to come back. And now, on this day in 1970, I was back and Hollywood wasn't there anymore. It was up for sale. Conglomerates were buying the studios and the computers were moving in, and no computer anywhere had ever made a work of art. Faceless people moved around, looking busy and efficient, talking about demographics, and yet . . . the industry, as Hollywood people always called their hybrid of business and art, was in trouble. The deepest, gravest trouble in its history. I turned and walked out of the Hairdressing Department. At the door a cage was locked across the "reception" counter. I walked to my dressing room once more. Across the entrance a sign had been erected: First Floor—Female Stars—Vacant.

That night I parked my car and walked around

Beverly Hills. It was damp and lush, the way the rich part of town usually is on a cool night. There were no people in sight—only shiny cars sprinkled with dew-drops. Several parties were in progress inside the warm plush homes. "For Sale" signs peeked above thousands of dollars' worth of elegantly trimmed underbrush. I had heard that four hundred and sixteen expensive homes were up for sale in Beverly Hills and Bel Air alone because the banks were about to foreclose. I'd heard that flocks of Hollywood's more successful and established creators were moving to the beach where they could set up "surf-staring" communities while waiting for the phone to ring. Days spread into long months for many who were feeling too paralyzed to attempt anything new or who were afraid to work without "up-front" money because everyone would then know they needed a job.

I walked for an hour, wondering what had really happened to Hollywood. Things had changed so much. People seemed either seventy or thirty. No one was in between. *Easy Rider* had seduced many into believing you could gross millions by spending only $400,000 to make a film (which made *Easy Rider*, in some ways, the most expensive film Hollywood ever produced). And the new crop of directors seemed to know a lot about films but very little about people. William Wyler, Billy Wilder, Robert Wise, Alfred Hitchcock, and other established directors seemed to be lumbering like dinosaurs over a terrain that required fleet feet rather than deep reflection.

The New Hollywood seemed to be all about how fast you could move, rather than what you understood, and in 1970, it bottomed out.

I walked into a party. A maid in a black uniform took

my wrap and a hostess greeted me warmly but without asking what I was doing these days. She was embarrassed and afraid that I might be embarrassed, and she used the same form on all the other guests.

"Mostly you see people's backs these days," someone said, "because no one really wants to hear what might be happening. It can only be worse." The hostess ushered me into the room and several people flashed glances of recognition at me, while going on with carefully constructed conversations. But there was no open, direct "Hello, how are you?" That was not something you asked in 1970; you might get an answer.

Yet, behind the "For Sale" signs and the foreclosures, the heated pools and colored fountains and catered squab dinners went on until the lights went out. The waiters, resplendent in black ties and cologne, did their best to help stave off reality, which was rushing in thick and fast now.

As though nothing was happening, I heard a producer predict, "Things will now revert to a healthy state of business. We'll learn how to keep costs down—that's all. And it'll enable us to clean out the deadwood and the unnecessary personnel." A circle of heads nodded in agreement. But when they spoke, tiny crevices around their mouths quivered with elaborately disguised tension. Who was the deadwood?

I walked toward the center of the room. Frank Sinatra raised a glass of Jack Daniels at me. He smiled that smile that charms the birds right out of trees and I wanted to stride up and interrogate him.

Nineteen seventy was the year Frank Sinatra turned to the Right. "Why did you do it, Frank?" I wanted to say. "Why did you come out for Ronald Reagan and why are you making noises about supporting Nixon? I used to kid you about being a closet king but did you have to come out?"

But before I could say anything, I was intercepted by a nice independent producer who had latched on to a nice young TV star who was working. And while he talked to me, I was thinking about my old friend Frank. What was so unusual about Sinatra being a Palm Springs dictator anyway? Hollywood always had a streak of the totalitarian in just about everything it did. The old moguls were essentially hard-fisted authoritarians who had created a system of linked dictatorships to control the creative people. We were supposed to be the children; mad, tempestuous, brilliant, talented, not terribly smart children. We were to be led, guided, manipulated, bought, sold, packaged, coddled, and tolerated. But we were not to be allowed to master our own destinies. Maybe that's what had burned Frank. Maybe he had been hurt once too often in his hard days before he learned how to wield power. Now he was supporting people who knew how to wield it more slickly and more broadly than he had ever imagined.

And his talent—his magnificent, generous talent—was being badly hurt along with his values. No, I had no problem about why Frank had made the switch. I pitied him for it, but I wasn't surprised. He had always loved gangsters, in a kind of romantic, theatrical way, as though he wanted really to be one. Now he was up there with the best of them. But I still liked him. At least he had the good grace to drop his smile and look away from me in embarrassed shame.

I walked toward Billy Wilder. He blinked like a mischievous toad and his face crinkled into a forced smile.

Billy was the master of eloquent cynicism; it was his stock in trade, but now it seemed to be eating him up. After a few opening amenities he launched into a familiar tirade against the public.

"Christ knows what they want," he said. "I can't seem to come up with the answer. The pictures that I think are sheer shit—they buy. So what do I know? I should go back to pimping in Berlin."

Billy was one of the most talented, abrasive minds I had ever worked with. But when I suggested that he was getting stale by hanging around Hollywood in his office, playing gin, and watching ball games on Sunday, he said that he only felt comfortable in Hollywood because he and his wife required hot and cold running carpets. The outside world was not for him. I wondered how long it would be before that kind of thinking caught up with him.

As I gazed around the walking guest list I slowly realized that half of the cast was from television. Television was keeping the studios alive and television was what had mortally wounded them—television and the American culture itself.

But Billy Wilder wasn't the only one who wondered what the American public wanted. The same question was perplexing the heads of all the studios. They used to be able to predict a success, gauging what the people of America wanted to see on a Saturday night. Not anymore. And worse, they had become frightened of the people out there who would ultimately decide their fates. Their own taste and judgment were shaky at best, and sometimes simply gone. Even when something was good they tended to self-destruct and tear it to shreds before it was properly launched. And you could feel that demorali-

zation permeating the creative community. Most everyone seemed to be on Automatic Pilot–Self-Destruct.

Everyone, that is, except the television people. The
men looked controlled and confident. The women had
stars in their eyes. It didn't seem to bother them at all
that they were engaged in the production of junk. Instead
they seemed to have accepted that as part of the deal,
saying essentially that it was better to work on junk
than not to work at all. I watched them as they moved
around that party. I wondered if it wasn't possible to do
television and be classy too.

I went to the powder room. The *Hollywood Reporter*,
a trade paper in town, was lying on top of the marble-
topped sink and I riffled through the pages. Production
was down. Grosses were "blah." But six new pilots were
being filmed for CBS. I worked my way to the back of
the paper and came to the real estate section. There was
one prominent ad, among three pages of other ads. It
contained a detailed description of a lovely Beverly Hills
mansion, complete with swimming pool, colored fountains, and tennis court. It was the house I was in.

I washed my hands and combed my hair and looked
again at the front page. There was nothing in the trade
papers about what had really gone wrong. Nothing about
Vietnam, or poverty, or racism, nothing about the way
the whole brave American dream seemed to be crumbling
around us. Nobody wrote that there would be no good
movies until we had a better country; and until the country felt better about itself it wasn't going to feel good
about going to see movies. Nobody in the movie business
seemed to want to make the connection, or cared to admit it. I went back to the party. A young television couple
was at the door, saying good night and explaining to the

host that they had to leave early because they were working in the morning. The movie people stayed on, with
the whiskey and the wine flowing as if nothing had happened to their world, as though it was still some evening
in the early sixties and they would be rich and famous
forever. I went and got my wrap and left as quietly as I
could. On the way home, driving through the cool night,
past all the dreams that the real estate men were offering
for sale, I started to think about television.

Three

Sir Lew Grade is an English tycoon, show business division, who has the ability to revive flagging enthusiasm simply by walking into a room. And if *you* walk into *his* room, he is likely to change your life. Give him a captive audience, and he can sell anything. He sold me television.

I went to see him one snowy day in London, knowing only the sketchiest details about him. I knew that he was chief executive and principal voting shareholder in the Associated Television Corporation Ltd., based in London, and he was said to be worth $400,000,000. I had seen his production of a TV special called "The Male of the Species" with Laurence Olivier, Michael Caine, and Paul Scofield, and thought it excellent. I knew he had started out poor, had become the Charleston champion of Europe in the 1920s, and was still capable of getting up on a table at the drop of a hat to display his virtuosity. But that wasn't knowing very much.

Now, on this snowy day, I could feel something very precise about the man, something that went beyond the beaming pink face, the short, squat body, the business-like belly that did not bounce. Sir Lew Grade struck me that day as a man who meant business about everything.

"What would you like, Shirley dear?" he asked, lighting an immense cigar. "Anything your little heart desires is yours."

He paced the spacious, stark office, relighting the

cigar, gesturing with a sort of ceremonial mischievous-
ness, knowing, like any good performer, just how charming and neatly effective he was with his repertoire of old
country humor. I can't remember everything he said: his
words were a blizzard, a storm, a Hurricane Zelda of
promises, dreams, visions. His head turned on his egg-
shaped body as he giggled and danced on the thick blue
carpets of that office over Marble Arch.

"Look, Shirley, let me be direct," he said. "I want to
capture a star, an American star who is a household
word. The fact that you are talented is super. But that's
not what interests me. What interests me about you,
Shirley, is your fame." He savored the word as he said it.

I felt my nose twitch.

"I want you because you're known to every housewife in America who eats meat patties when the TV
set is on in the living room. I want you. And if you
like working with me, then I know you'll act as my
agent, getting other big name stars to come here too.
You'll be the great example to all of them. I'll get
them to move to this side of the Atlantic, and, together,
we'll help raise the level of television in America."

I didn't know whether he meant all that, but I was
really concerned about the apparently all-pervasive mediocrity of the medium. I didn't really know much about
television, but I was determined that if I took the plunge,
I wanted to be in something that was not going to insult
the average American. With some luck it might be
possible to create a series that was well-written, hand-
somely mounted, finely directed, and well-acted. It would
take place in the real world, and not in the vanilla ice-
cream fantasy land where so many situation comedies
took place. In fact, it shouldn't be a "situation comedy"

at all. It could be a show that moved people, cheered them up, made them believe in the essential humanity of themselves and others. And it could mean something, especially if it showed a woman doing more in her life than simply pampering a slow-witted husband, dealing with a mess of children, or accepting unhappiness with stoic good grace. I thought we could center it on a woman who was a professional reporter who wandered the four corners of the world without the protection of men, a woman who enjoyed her life and didn't have to call home for advice. I thought women would be able somehow to live vicariously through such a character, and that men would admire her and not be threatened by her. I talked to Sir Lew about some of those things. He talked about money.

His secretary poked her head through an adjoining door. "Lunch is ready, Sir Lew," she said. And we moved on to a table where caviar and melon and assorted fruit and cheese were laid out buffet-style. On the way to the table, we passed his desk: it was bone clean.

"I want to pay you more than any American network can afford to pay you," Sir Lew said, watching me eat smoked salmon from a silver tray. "You'll help stimulate employment here, and I'll work out a movie deal too. You would shoot only four months a year on television, and I'll finance two pictures a year for you, on any subject that interests you."

As he spoke, his eyes never left me. I felt strangely out of time. I told him that I had doubts, that I didn't think famous faces were enough anymore for television audiences which were growing more and more sophisticated. Americans had learned a lot about the world through television, had seen war in Vietnam, starvation in Biafra, riots, invasions, shootings of students, assassinations of leaders; all in living color, while they changed the kid's diapers.

"There's still hero worship in America," I said, "but I don't think being a star is enough."

"You're wrong, Shirley," he replied. "People like to watch people they already know. It relaxes them, makes them feel comfortable. They haven't the time to get acquainted with new faces; they have too much else to do with their lives. Believe me, it wouldn't matter if you read the telephone book."

Two hours moved by, with the snow still falling and Sir Lew still talking. We talked about films, commercials, his wife, Kathy, his son in private school, his attitude toward money (A little girl once asked him if two and two made four. Sir Lew answered: "Buying or selling?"). The phone didn't ring once.

At the end of the fourth uninterrupted hour, he summed up, and added a few points:

"Think hard about what I'm offering, Shirley. But don't take long to make up your mind. One year from now, because of the new FCC ruling cutting a half hour from prime time, there won't be many time slots open. Do you realize how few opportunities there will be for new shows, or offers like the one I'm now making you? It'll be murder. Murder. So listen carefully. You must make up your mind now in order to have time to prepare for a show that will go on the air a year from now. There's no time to waste. And I'll finance any pictures you want to make, and if you want to direct too, well, you've got it."

Sir Lew walked me to the elevator, saying hello to everybody in his office, calling them by first name. The building seemed to be his home. And his employees treated him as if he were some wonderful, respected, powerful, and rich uncle. I went downstairs, thinking how odd life was; the movies didn't want the big stars anymore, but TV wanted us to bail them out. It was all very strange. On the street the snow was up to my ankles. I trudged along, thinking. I knew my professional life had changed.

We agreed to meet three days later at his office in the Desilu Studios. That would give me time to assimilate what he had said. I walked him to his long car and watched him disappear down the driveway. Assimilate what he had said? What had he said? Oh yes, I was to play a girl photographer named Shirley Logan and work in an office in London and have a boyfriend who was anti-Establishment and a boss who wasn't and the conflict would be between the two men while I looked on as an arbiter and kept the peace.

I went inside and made myself a gin and tonic.

Three days later, on schedule, I met with Sheldon in his office at Desilu. The lot and its buildings, which used to house RKO pictures, now looked like all TV buildings: transient, impermanent, without the solidity of buildings that are devoted to the making of motion pictures. It was as if even the structures knew they could be canceled in the morning.

Sheldon's blonde secretary, Skippy, led me to the office, where cigar smoke hung in the room and the air conditioner was making so much noise I could hardly hear him. Sheldon, dressed now in blue suede jacket with matching shirt, ushered me to a chair.

I asked him if he would mind not smoking the cigar. It was a problem from my childhood, I explained, and told him about a day back in Virginia when I was twelve, and my father, a real estate salesman then, left me to take care of a house he had up for sale. There were no visitors and I had nothing to do. Except that Dad had left a box of cigars on the floor. I lit one up. It made me sick. Then a customer finally arrived, and I showed him the house, explaining all the details of the mortgage and the first trust and the rest of it. He wanted to buy the house and I told him to talk to Dad. The customer said: "You sold it, you know." Yes, I said, and Dad promised me a commission if I did a good job. The customer laughed and went away to see Dad while I threw up from the cigar. Three days later the man and his wife bought the house, but my father didn't give me a commission.

"So as far as I'm concerned, Sheldon," I said, after narrating this tale, "cigars stand for bullshit."

I was laughing as I said it, but Sheldon immediately put out the cigar.

And so we started. Sheldon said that the first step was to call in some writers and kick around ideas. That sounded nice and loose to me, and I suggested that he bring them all up to the house, where I could cook, and the writers could get to know me, see the way I move, hear the way I speak.

"I'd like to be myself on television," I said. "You know, the real me, instead of acting somebody I've already been in films."

I must have said something wrong. Sheldon rolled his cold cigar between his teeth and looked at me for a long beat.

"See those leather-bound scripts up there?" he said. There were rows of them, all neatly labeled from "I Spy" to the "Dick Van Dyke Show." "My hits," he said, his lips curling like the Runyon character he used to play. "I could buy and sell the networks. I've turned my expertise into millions and I've learned how to manipulate the men of television so that they do what's best for *them*. You have to know how. I know how."

The idea of bringing writers to the house had vanished, like the cigar smoke, and I sat looking at him. He asked

me what I thought of the show he had outlined that day
on the patio, and I told him I didn't really care a whole
lot about playing a girl whose boyfriend thinks one way
while her boss thinks another.

"I'd like to play a girl who thinks *her* way, Sheldon,"
I said. "And who doesn't give too much of a crap which
way either of the fellas thinks."

"Crap?"

"Oh. *Yeah.*"

He filed that away somewhere, and started pacing the
office. He explained that the "Shirley Logan" character
would also run an orphanage in London, "filled with
international-type orphans that somehow cross your
path." This would bring me sympathy, "especially if you
want to play one of those independent, aggressive women
who operate on their own. You can't just be independent
on TV. You have to pay some price and that price is
children."

I should have known right then that we were in
trouble. Sheldon clearly felt that independent women
threatened TV audiences; I acknowledged that television
was the the most intimate medium, that performers on
television were like the house guests, but that was the
very reason I wanted to play a woman as close to myself
as possible. I wanted to be myself on television; I had
spent a long time thinking about what that self was, and
finally had the courage to expose it.

"If I play something I don't believe," I said, "how
can I expect them to believe it out there?"

Sheldon never had time to answer. Ed Vane, head of
nighttime programming for the American Broadcasting
Company, walked in with a folder marked "Shirley Mac-
Laine Samplings" and started to explain that ABC's mar-

ket and audience researchers had discovered that the people polled gave me high marks on humanitarianism.

"On what?"

"On humanitarianism," Vane said confidently. "The guidance reactors tested indicate a high response to your quality of helping others. Your vulnerability quotient was extremely high too."

It was all there in the research, Vane said, some of it actually done by wiring human beings with metal conductors, "which are placed on specific pulse regions of the body in order to ascertain emotional response from the public." The people tested didn't want me to be married on the show, and almost all, Vane explained, wanted me to have romantic adventures.

Sheldon was looking out the window and listening. As Vane wound down, Sheldon turned and asked us if we wanted coffee. Vane said no, apologized, and then told us he had to leave for another meeting.

"I always have a problem with these experts in mechanical evaluation," Sheldon said, after Vane had left. "Even the nature of questioning the public as to its preferred tastes is fallacious."

He talked a while about the mechanical problems of shooting a twenty-four-episode series when twelve of the episodes would be set in foreign countries, something Sir Lew had promised me. Sheldon thought it was a waste of time and money to go to the far corners of the world for a TV show, what with language problems, clearances, logistical details.

"The public watches people," he said, "not foreign locations."

I knew what he meant, and to some extent agreed. But I had a notion that the secret of *this* TV show would be in integrating the performers with the place, so that the foreign locations were not simply a fancy backdrop. I wanted to travel light, with a small crew, and respond to the foreign environment as directly as possible.

"That way," I said, "we have people *and* locations going for us."

Sheldon stared at me.

"What kind of stories can we do?" he asked.

I suggested that there were plenty of stories, that Shirley Logan could even be involved in the same sort of adventures I had been involved in. I had written a book about some of those adventures, and had sent a copy to Sheldon. I asked him if he had had time to read it. Yes, he said. What did he think?

"Revealing," he said. "Revealing." And rolled the cold cigar.

"Sheldon," I said at last. "Do you like to travel?"

"If there's a reason."

"I don't mean professionally. I mean personally. Do you like to go places?"

"I'm very widely traveled," he said. "You know that."

"But do you like it?"

"I don't like being away from my grandchildren," he said. "I've made about twelve million dollars. I don't see any point in doing it the hard way anymore."

The meeting was going downhill, but there didn't seem to be much I could do about it. We started talking about Shirley Logan's sex life. I suggested that it wasn't necessary to tie her down to one boyfriend in London, that she could have friends all over the world, and if she wanted to go to bed with one of them every once in a while, well, that would be all right too. In other words, this reporter-photographer on *this* show should be a free woman.

"Then you mean you want to make her a slut," Sheldon said.

"A free woman is a slut?" I said. That really stopped me. Now *I* got up from the chair.

"This female liberation thing," Sheldon said. "You know, it's a real threat to television."

There it was. I wondered how many times in how many offices the same words were being spoken that year, and how many men were making professional decisions based on their personal feelings about women. Sheldon was probably a decent man, certainly a successful one, and if the series worked, this was the beginning of a professional relationship that would last five years. But now we knew each other better, and were probably skeptical of each other and of the future. He was an expert in television. I was a woman who knew what she wanted to do on television, or, more precisely, what I didn't want to do. Neither of us could be sure who was right. I went out into the strange transient lot, and somewhere near the gate my stomach turned over.

Five

"SHIRLEY'S WORLD," as the series was called, became for me an experience something akin to what Vietnam must have been for Kennedy, Johnson, and Nixon. You begin by sticking a big toe into the water and before you know what has happened, you are up to your neck in a cesspool. Later, you can never really pinpoint the moment when you could have, or should have, gotten out. To be involved with television was devastating and revealing but the experience was even more important to me personally because it made clear to me my own struggling, indecisive values.

Early on, when the first scripts had come in, I had called my agent to complain. I told him it just wasn't going to work, the scripts were terrible. I was playing a nosy, irritating, empty-minded little banana head, who goes around the world bothering people. Worse, the people Shirley Logan bothered were even lower on the human scale than she was. The Italians pinched her, the Arabs stole, the Chinese were stupid and mercenary, the Japanese were buck-toothed, secretive Mr. Motos, the Irish were drunks, the Spaniards were lazy liars. I told him I wanted out. There was a long pause.

"Shirl," he said, "I gotta tell you. There's more involved with this series than I think you realize. Riding on your face right now, I would say—conservatively is, oh, $20,000,000 with advertising and air time combined."

That was a very large figure, and I tried to maintain

my composure. I asked him if it would be possible to postpone the start date of the series, from September to January, or until the following season, giving us more time to prepare decent scripts. He said that would be impossible.

"You can't move around start dates like you do in movies," my agent said. "And besides, these men in television are different human beings. They're not men of courage. They're scared shitless—all of them. I know of *no* exceptions. You can't even *discuss* postponement because they have absolute air dates they must meet."

I told him that I was worried about Sheldon Leonard, and how the scripts seemed to confirm my fears, but my agent told me the facts of life. Sheldon was the executive producer; they were paying me the highest salary in television history, because they trusted *him*. I would have to give it more of a chance. The scripts were only first drafts. It happened in every series. By the time the third and fourth drafts came in, everything would be the way I wanted it. "Relax," he said. "I understand."

I went to New York, made two movies financed by Sir Lew, and waited for the second and third drafts. They were not better: some, in fact, were worse.

In March 1971, I flew to England. Maybe, I thought, we can make this work when we get it on its feet. But I really didn't believe it. Cesspool-wise, I was up to my knees already.

The house I lived in was rented by Sir Lew. It was large and sprawling and very English, filled with antiques and set on a large, quiet estate in Windsor Park. It was a half hour from the Pinewood Studios and forty-five minutes from London. There was a full-time chauffeured

Rolls-Royce at my disposal, a butler and a cook and a gardener, and Sir Lew had taken a five-year lease on the place, because as he put it, "that's at least how long your series will run." Sir Lew had outdone himself.

At the studio, there was a newly decorated dressing room, complete with bedroom and bath, and a small kitchenette. Everything seemed to be first class, including the crew. I just wished the scripts were of as high a quality as everything else.

Crews are shrewd and perceptive people. They can smell a successful, well-conceived project, and they are rarely wrong. They can also smell trouble.

This refined sense of smell comes from self-interest and self-preservation; the success of a show determines whether the crew will have jobs. And "Shirley's World" was an enormous attempt at success. If we made it, hundreds and hundreds of British workers would have jobs, and A.T.V. and Sir Lew Grade would be firmly established in the world of American television. Those first weeks, everyone talked about how much money was being spent on each episode, and Sheldon gave some interviews boasting that it was the most expensive series in television history, and therefore would be successful. Because of this talk, and the five-year potential, many crew members gave up motion picture work to join the series.

They performed magnificently. They were imaginative, quick, humorous. For about two weeks.

Then the word started to get around about the scripts. They were coming in now, so that each department could prepare for future episodes. And I could feel, almost taste, the change in atmosphere. When an American is stunned by bad taste or simple mediocrity, the

response is usually direct. An Englishman behaves **dif-**
ferently. He is less willing to verbalize his feelings, **trying**
somehow to observe decorum at all costs.

I could feel the erosion begin around me, as Sheldon
stood at the top of the production, remote and mono-
lithic. Set designers grew unhappy because they had to
build sets for scripts that weren't finished. The costume
and hair people had read the scripts, and it was hard for
them to be creative when their own attitudes were not
positive. The actors had the most difficult time of all,
since they were required to say things they would not
possibly say if they were not being paid well to say them.
At one point, ABC sent word that they had a higher
sponsor reaction to the potential of my series than any
other planned for that season. The sponsors seemed to
be the only people involved who had not read the scripts.

In April, as we prepared to make our first trip to a
foreign location, Hong Kong, it had dawned on some of
us, slowly, a day at a time, that we had a disaster on our
hands.

Six

To me Hong Kong had always been one of the loveliest places in the world. I loved the smell of it, the smell of the sea and thousands of noonday meals wafting through the air, accompanied by the singsong of Cantonese voices and the clink of chopsticks. I loved the clean laundry hung from bamboo poles on all the balconies, and the rickshaw men shouting their availability at each intersection while the proprietors of a hundred jewelry shops enticed the passers-by to treat themselves to tax-free pearls and original designs in jewelry. Hong Kong was a shopper's paradise in the old days, a place where you could go broke saving money. I loved the hustle and the feeling that you were always getting something for nothing. The Cantonese understood the psychology of money and how it operated in every nationality of human being. They knew the German attitude, the Russian, the Japanese. They had to, because Hong Kong was an international port; its only purpose was bargains.

I used to take off my jacket on the streets and feel the humid spices settle onto my skin. There was no way ever to feel completely dry in Hong Kong and I admired the silk pajamas of the peasant women, feeling awkward and hot in my Western slacks with matching blouse and jacket. I learned to love material that billowed with the slightest breeze, and often wanted to melt into the teeming millions and the lilting Chinese landscape, and soak up that part of the world I loved so much.

Sheldon had preceded us by a week and was happily ensconced at the Hong Kong race track when we arrived, accompanied by a crew of thirty-five, including grips, cameramen, hairdressers, electricians, assistants, drivers, costume people, and logistic experts. It looked like the invasion of Okinawa. Sheldon said the Chinese and Japanese episodes were marvelous and I should consider the foreign locations a new beginning.

I was elated, until I read the scripts. They were worse than any so far. To add to my humiliation, many of the Hong Kong press people had managed to read them too. During a press conference they asked if I had OK'd the writing of the series. Their expressions were incredulous and the tone of their voices decidedly pejorative. I had difficulty answering. How could I explain that I hated the entire experience but was waiting for fourth drafts because I didn't want to be sued?

There was, in fact, no real point in arguing over the scripts anymore. Sheldon only smiled tolerantly and told me not to worry. Then he left us and went ahead to Japan. The situation was hopeless. I could feel myself searching for a way to get through it—I would think only about *where* I was, I thought, not *what* I was doing there.

I would focus only on Hong Kong, a place I loved as much as any place in the world. Then I realized how blind the series had made me. If I thought the series was bad it was nothing compared to what had happened to Hong Kong.

It hit me first one afternoon as I stood on the deck of the Hong Kong Star Ferry. Quite suddenly, I felt trapped. The crisp ocean air was soiled with pollutants. On the mountain roads of Repulse Bay, a truck stalled and belched black smoke, and I felt my stomach tighten. The sounds of automobile traffic, bumper-to-bumper and screeching angrily, drowned out the old haunting fugue of the harbor foghorns. I looked out at the jade green hills which had once touched the placid harbor waters like those in an ancient Chinese scroll, but the view was blocked by new skyscrapers. Once there had been jagged footpaths carved through those hills, along which lovers climbed to reach windy heights and plan the future. But they were gone too. The bulldozers had snatched away the rocks and the lovers too.

During the day, I couldn't breathe on the street, and longed for evening, when the noise and pollution would subside. We shot our silly scenes on those streets, and at night lying alone in bed, I thought about the thousands of babies being born every month into families that already lived six in a room. Maybe that was what it was all about. Maybe there were too many of us on the earth, and, as a result, mediocrity was certain to be our lot. In the old days, the jewelry and bags and beaded material of Hong Kong had been finely sewn, handmade, given the lavish attention of craftsmen. Now the products were tacky-looking and sloppily made, as the dwindling number of craftsmen were engulfed by the demands of the swelling numbers of customers. The same thing was happening in television. We were apparently expected to appeal to the largest numbers of people, which meant figuring out the lowest common denominator.

Perhaps mediocrity *was* more salable than quality. Maybe Sheldon was right about the series and the Hong Kong salesmen were right about their wares. They were both interested in numbers—big numbers—rather than quality. I would get out of bed, move to the picture window of the hotel room, and look out past the lights of the choking city, out to the great black strip of land that lay mysterious and silent on the other side. Out there was the People's Republic of China. I wondered who was up at this hour of the night and what they were thinking about us.

After three weeks in Hong Kong, we moved on to Japan. The Japanese scripts were worse than the Chinese. All the Orientals walked around with buck teeth and spoke Pidgin English and I was either Charlie Chan in a skirt, or Miss Lonelyhearts. Meanwhile, Sheldon left Japan and returned to England, repeating his disappearing act so he wouldn't have to discuss scripts. Before he left he gave an interview explaining that he didn't want mine to be a "women's lib" series, and he told me he didn't want me to use my show as a soapbox. I assured him that I could think of better ways to influence people. As the show deteriorated, the English production people began angling for the best offices and the fanciest furniture in anticipation of our return to London. I guess they figured they'd get what they could while they could.

However, all of this seemed trivial when I realized the changes that had taken place in Japan. I had been away only two years, but in that brief period this nation of nature-loving Buddhists seemed to have surrendered to technology. Parks, once bursting with flowers, were being torn up in favor of factories. The countryside had virtually disappeared, and the area from Yokohama to Tokyo had been converted into one huge, smoking urban complex.

As we moved from location to location filming our stupid stories, I saw and heard and smelled all the symbols of the new Japan: blaring horns, dense smoke, tides of people, desecrated temples, stalled lanes of traffic, brown poisoned air, bewildered school children, and the inevitable shortened tempers. Somehow, that was the worst of all. Something terrible must happen for the Japanese to lose their tempers and now they seemed to be losing their tempers with every contact.

They were also being consciously rude, not simply to each other, but to foreigners as well, something that would have been unheard of in the old days. One afternoon, I walked in to the beauty shop of the New Otani Hotel to ask for the use of a shampoo bowl. I had been in and out of the hotel for years, and knew Mr. Otani, the owner. There were two customers in the shop, and five empty sinks.

"Not possible," the proprietress snapped.

I told her I would greatly appreciate it, it would not take long, but I was filming a scene outside, I had my own hairdresser with me to do the washing and my own shampoo. If I had to use a hotel shower for the shampoo, my make-up would come off.

"No," she said, without explanation.

I asked for a phone, but she did not answer. So I picked up the phone and asked the operator for Mr. Otani.

"Maybe Mr. Otani will know where there is a bowl available," I said to the proprietress. "I'll just tell him there are none available here."

"It won't help," she said severely. "I am Mrs. Otani."

I hung up the phone and left. Something terrible

was going on, and I didn't even know how to ask the questions that might lead to the answers.

Our house in Shibuya section of Tokyo looked the same, nestled cosily against the garden that my husband, Steve Parker, had built by hand. But the leaves of the bamboo were hanging limp in the brown air. The carp were dying in the fish pond, as soot coated the surface of the water. We had to release more water through the waterfall to drown out the sound of the street traffic.

I called some Western friends who had lived in Japan since the end of the war. "We're leaving, Shirley," they said. "It's out of control. Even if they tried to reverse the situation right now, they would still have ten years of industrial contracts to fulfill. You know what that means. It's lost. It's over. We're leaving."

One day when we were not shooting, I took a car and tried to find the countryside. My ears popped and the temperature fell, but otherwise, I wouldn't have known I was in the mountains. Everything was industrialized highway: no peaks, no rolling hills. When I reached the mountain resort of Iwahara I found myself in a crush of people also looking for a way to escape Tokyo. Wave after wave of humans pushed against each other in an area that twelve years earlier had been completely silent. Even the trees seemed to me to shrink from the masses of people shoveling food into their mouths, trampling the grass to death, picking and choosing vacation souvenirs, and licking quickly manufactured frozen ice-milk cones.

In the temples, giant statues of Buddha stared down on man fouling his own nest.

I left Iwahara and drove deeper and higher into the

mountains, hoping that there, far from the city and the worship of the Gross National Product, I would find some of the old culture still intact.

At a quaint Japanese inn, a mama-san in old style kimono ushered me in, bowing her welcome in the traditional way. In the late afternoon, she invited me to join them for the green tea ceremony. Years before, I had tried to learn the green tea ceremony, and had failed. It was so complicated, with such precise and intricate requirements of ritual, that as soon as I would master one movement, I'd forget the one before it. In essence, the ceremony involved the turning of the green tea cup so many times in one direction, with the fingers placed gently and precisely around the rim of the cup. The spooning of the green tea powder was itself almost impossible for a Westerner to master. You use a narrow curved dipper of smooth polished wood, and with no convenient bowl to the curved bottom, it is necessary to choose the exact amount of powder. Otherwise it will spill, and to a Japanese spilling anything is uncouth and rude.

I knelt before the mama-san on the woven tatami mat as she prepared for the ceremony. Behind the *shoji* screen, a waterfall trickled gently. For a moment I felt as if I had traveled back through time two hundred years.

With quiet, predetermined movements she began to handle and turn the cup counterclockwise. Her eyes were cast downward, assuming the exact degree of ceremonial decorum. Her feet, covered with spotless *tabi* (Japanese socks) neatly overlapping each other, peeked out from under her kimono of beige and white brocade. A low lacquer cabinet housing all the ingredients for the ceremony stood beside her. I sat enthralled. She was ready to mix the tea. With a ritualistically gentle reach she opened the cabinet and took a Lipton tea bag out of a box, placed it in the cup and poured hot boiling water from a plastic bottle over it! At that moment the *sensi* (teacher and master) of the inn pulled back the *shoji* screen that was separating us. He was lying on a vibrator chair watching television.

I sipped the tea quietly, and after a while thanked them, excused myself, and went back to the car.

I carried one final image with me from Japan. One morning at dawn, while I was traveling to the location, I saw a traffic policeman etched against the magenta tint of the sunrise. He was stooped, leaning over a low rock wall, tending a small potted plant. Gently he caressed the leaves of the red flower. His eyes were proud as he patted the flower pot and straightened up, looking down at his own small and private garden. Then he reached behind the low rock wall and pulled out a gas mask. The flower trembled in the morning traffic as we rolled by him, and he pulled the gas mask over his face and went to work.

Seven

WITH LOCATION SHOOTING completed we returned to London and a fine English summer, bright with sun and the smell of fresh-cut grass. But there were clouds gathering over Pinewood Studios, and they grew increasingly dark and ugly. Sheldon had gone back to America from England, disappearing again, and he made it clear that he was staying there. He communicated with us by recorded cassettes. Since we were without a producer now, I complained to Lew Grade and was promised that one would come soon. I would climb into the car and be driven through the lovely countryside to the studio and every morning upon arrival, I would ask whether we had a producer yet. The weeks dragged on, but no one ever came.

All around me, I could feel morale disintegrating. All departments broke down. Some of the motion picture technicians who had joined us when the series was a promising idea went back to motion pictures. I went to see the film we had shot in Asia, and it was uncuttable. Worse, I looked depressed on the screen; the contamination had infected my own performance. It was the worst thing that could happen to an actor.

Without a producer, the weight of responsibility fell upon me. I could sense the whispering that was going on, as everyone looked for a place to lay the blame. A power struggle began among those who thought the series might last five years no matter how bad it was.

One director started ordering furniture for Sheldon's vacant office and began acting as though he were Sheldon's replacement. The ABC brass arrived in England, heard the stories, listened to my complaints, and viewed the film.

"We're just glad it's not out of focus," one of them said. We all laughed, bleakly.

There was still no producer. I waited another week.

Finally, one morning I packed my suitcases, went out to the airport, boarded a plane for America, and quit the series. Sir Lew nearly had a coronary. Until then, he had not taken my warnings and objections seriously, telling me that my "fame and status" would overcome all problems of quality. But this was different. He even called British Customs to find out what mood I was in when I left London.

I shut myself into my New York apartment, read some books, watched some television, and slept late in the mornings. Every five minutes the phone would ring, but I didn't answer. I left word with my agent that I was talking to nobody until I had a producer. It took two and a half days.

The man was Ron Rubin, a bearded and mustached, thirty-five-year-old six-footer, who was wearing a madras shirt the first time I saw him, and an expression of sheer incredulity. The year before, he had produced an ABC series called "Room 222" and had been in the business for ten years. But as we shook hands, his thick black eyebrows started to knit. He had just left the ABC projection room, after having flown overnight from California.

"I might as well get right to the point," he said, "because I'm too tired to do otherwise. These shows are terrible. I don't know what Shirley Logan is all about and the stories are ridiculous." He paused for a beat. "Now what do you want me to do?"

I wanted him to save the show. I wanted him to make the character come to life. I wanted him to get good writers working on good scripts and good directors to direct them. I wanted him to produce a show in which a real woman lived in the real world, and had some fun and adventure while she was at it. In short, I wanted him to make the proverbial silk purse out of a sow's ear.

What he did do was to fly immediately to England, with me on another plane, and start work. He threw out the scripts for twenty-six planned episodes, an investment of $235,000, and then threw out the three dismal Hong Kong episodes. For the first time Sir Lew blinked. I wasn't certain what it all meant yet, but at least there was movement. The junk was gone; it remained to be seen whether it could be replaced with something good.

Meanwhile, Sheldon had been told that he was through with the show. He didn't see it that way, and of course he had a contract. Diplomatically, he checked into a hospital in Los Angeles for a few days' rest, and sent word that he wouldn't be coming to England for a while.

Now the pressure of time began to assert itself. We were two weeks away from our second location jaunt, probably to Spain, and we did not have a single shootable script. Worse, the September 15 air date was becoming real now, instead of some mythical date in the distant future. The first assistant director quit. The costume, props, scenic design, and hairdressing departments came to a standstill. They were all waiting for new scripts from the new writers.

And that meant they were waiting for Ron Rubin, the man everybody expected to bring off the miracle. But he was having problems. Around London, the show had acquired such a bad reputation that it was difficult to get good writers or directors. Rubin stayed in his office. He never came down to the sound stages to introduce himself to the crew as the new producer; maybe he knew something I didn't know. The English sharks were politicking all around him, currying favor. He told me that he turned blue every afternoon about three, because there were no windows in his office. I wondered why he wasn't purple.

One afternoon, shortly before he turned blue, Rubin came to my dressing room for a long talk. After three weeks in England, he was heavily depressed. He didn't know how to handle the lies and the demoralization. He found himself "settling" all the time, he said, allowing dialogue lines and unresolved plot points to slide by in the scripts, because he couldn't fight the mediocrity of the people working with him. It was a war of attrition and they were wearing him down.

I found myself trying to reassure Ron Rubin, trying to build up his morale, placate him, and tell him that things were not as bad as he thought. In short I found myself telling him the things he was supposed to be telling me. A week later, he quit and went home to America. I knew that day that it was all over for the show.

On September 15, the first show went on the air in America, while we were working at Pinewood. Sheldon Leonard made a brief ceremonial trip to London to be with us when we got the news. I was doing my best with a dull scene, when I saw him walk on the set.

When the scene was over, I went over to say hello. He was breathing deeply, the corners of his mouth quivering.

"Well, kid, stop worrying," he said. "You're the only horse in the race this season."

I didn't know what to say. The other horses didn't worry me. It was the race itself. I didn't sleep that night. But I didn't call America either.

Then, the next morning, my publicity man called from New York with a review from a Canadian paper. It was the first word on the show, and the word was smash. "Sensational . . . fresh . . . original." I stood in the dressing room, looking out at the studio grounds. I couldn't believe what I had heard. Maybe I had been wrong. Maybe all the demoralization and pain and self-questioning had been my fault; maybe none of it had been necessary; maybe Sheldon and the ABC people and Lew Grade had been right all along. That night I fell asleep hoping beyond hope that I had been as wrong as an actress can be.

The crew was in early the next day, awaiting the arrival of Sheldon, who would have the first hard news of the American response to the first episode of the show. "What have you heard?" I was asked. Nothing yet. Nothing real. We went outside to shoot in the bright sunlight, and then Sheldon arrived with his familiar tweed elegance. I wanted the news, good or bad, at the same time everyone else heard it, and we crowded around Sheldon, searching his face for telltale signs. He took a deep breath.

"Ladies and gentlemen," he said, "it looks like we have the comedy smash of the season." It was as if our whole group exhaled at once. "I've checked with my sources," he went on, "my own private Nielsen ratings, and we clobbered the opposition. The show has been described as alternately charming, funny, delightful, a breath of fresh air, and a triumph." He smiled. "I'd like to thank you for your patience, your hard work, your talent . . . And . . . congratulations."

My corset was digging into my stomach and I thought I was going to croak right there. My God, we had made it. It had worked. We had made it, goddammit. The crew broke into applause, seeing five future Christmases laid out before them, and we all went back to work. For the first time since the series started, I was funny all day.

At the end of the day, bubbling with excitement, feeling that if the audience liked the first show they would love the shows that came from good scripts, I rushed back to the dressing room. It was time to have a drink with everybody, to call friends, to laugh. I went to my dressing room to change.

My secretary was on a long-distance call, talking to my publicity man in New York. Her face was the color of chalk and she was speaking in a whisper. She looked up apprehensively, and motioned to me with the phone.

"Shirl," she said, "I'd better let Joe tell you."

I felt panic skitter through me.

"What do you mean?" I said.

"You'd better ask him."

I picked up the phone and asked him what was going on.

"We just got the overnight ratings in New York," he said. "I can't understand it. Even if they hated the first show, it would seem they would tune in just to see *you*, especially with the publicity campaign, which was terrific."

"Well, what is it, Joe?" I said. "Sheldon says it's a smash. Isn't that true? His people said it was the best thing on television in the last five years."

"Are you kidding? *His* people? Who the fuck did he talk to? Shirl, the ratings are a disaster and the reviews are worse. I don't even want to read them to you."

The bottom dropped out. We talked a little longer, about what the other shows did (Anthony Quinn and Henry Fonda were on the same night as I was on ABC and they were wiped out too). I told him I would call him back. Then I dialed Sheldon at his hotel.

"Mr. Leonard checked out this afternoon, Miss," the operator's voice said. "He left no forwarding address. Sorry."

So was I. I walked into the dressing room and closed the door and lay down on the bed, staring at the ceiling. After a while I fell asleep.

It was a chill autumn day when I left London. The chestnut trees in the back garden were a blazing orange. And wet clouds, heavy with rain, moved majestically overhead. For weeks, as I lived the sad little life of Shirley Logan, I had stopped seeing nature, and I suddenly wished that I could stay through an entire English winter, watching the seasons change, along with the leaves and the trees and the wet grass. But instead, I was going home.

"Maybe today seems so beautiful because yesterday was terrible," my driver, Reg, said, looking at me through the rearview mirror. "That's the way life is too."

Maybe it was. As I flew across the ocean, I wondered what people in the movie business would think of me now, and how my friends would talk about me. Would they whisper about my humiliation and my bad judgment, with napkins discreetly covering their mouths? For a week, I stayed in my apartment in New York and didn't see anybody. Or let anybody see me. Then, one afternoon, I went around the corner to my neighborhood grocery.

"Hey, how are ya, Miss MacLaine," the grocer said. "Long time no see. You been away, huh?"

"Yes," I said, "I've been all over the place."

"Oh, yeah," he said, "doing that TV show, right? I hear it's not as good as your book. I loved the book."

I asked him what specifically he thought about the show, whether the foreign countries were attractive, whether *it looked good.*

"To tell you the truth," he said, "I never seen the show. Mister Whitney, the writer around the corner, he told me. But he only saw one. You know, to me everything you do is OK. Listen, how about some of these berries. Real fresh. Just in . . ."

I bought three pounds of berries and on the way out I reached over and kissed him.

Then I remembered something my agent had said once: "The one good thing about having a disaster, kid, is that nobody sees it."

Eight

NEW YORK is the perfect town for getting over a disappointment, a loss, or a broken heart. Some people find it cruel and lonely. To me it was a transfusion, mostly because it was real. In New York you can be sure of what's happening—good or bad. There's no way to cover or disguise it, and in those weeks that followed my return to America, I plunged into the city as if I'd never been there before.

It was just before Christmas. I caroused with my friends, hung around Shubert Alley during intermissions, window-shopped along Madison and Lexington Avenues until my feet hurt. On a given day I would mosey into Serendipity for a frozen mocha; plunder the shirt shop at Bloomingdale's; walk to the Village and back until I reached Beekman Place at sunset and breathed in the smell of the East River. Later I'd tumble into Elaine's on Eighty-eighth Street and Second Avenue just to see who was around.

I would stay up all night listening to my journalist friends, who would tell me all the inside news that wasn't fit to print. I went to every boring intellectual cocktail party in town, and cleaned out my mind later by listening to New York cabdrivers talk about everything from Mayor Lindsay to spaceships. I would stand around my corner market, in the city where a seed was lucky to sprout, and listen to conversations about juicy, red-ripe tomatoes and hard-to-get artichokes, and I loved the neighborhood feeling that was still possible in the large, dirty, human city of eight million.

The city was supposed to be a disaster, but its flow of raw energy made me bounce again. I wanted it all: the smell of the oil fumes on the crosstown bus, the crowds piling out of the subways, the lofty buildings that were New York man's loftiest monument to himself. I wanted to eat every broiled Maine lobster that could be set before me, and every steak too. I wanted to sit in my apartment for hours, watching all the news shows, and eating cinnamon buns from the automat. Nowhere in the world was the news so well covered. Nowhere in the world could you buy a cinnamon bun from a hole in the wall.

New York was the center of communications for more reasons than Rockefeller Center. It was a city where it was impossible not to communicate. If you went down to the corner for a loaf of bread, chances were that you would meet *and talk* with at least two people. New York was the only city I knew in the world where you could be desperately lonely at nine in the morning, crossing the street for a bagel at Gristede's, and find that seven hours later you were drinking Irish coffee at P. J. Clarke's with all the friends you had inherited along the way.

But soon after those first giddy weeks home, I began to feel American again. Mixing in with the late-night talk at Elaine's, after all the gossip about who was sleeping with whom—and why—darker themes crept in: race, Kent State, the growing conservatism of the Supreme Court, the government attacks on the free press, crime, women's liberation, and of course, the darkest theme of all—Vietnam. I discovered that returning to America was like returning to a dear, ailing friend. Something terrible was going wrong.

I began to receive new movie scripts. But they weren't
about anything real. They seemed to have nothing to do
with the world as it existed. It seemed as though creative
people didn't know what to create, and the money
people didn't want anything that was even remotely con-
troversial. Creators were told that shows about the war
were unfinanceable, shows about independent women
would turn off the male audiences, and shows with social
significance were not what the audience wanted to see.
That left sex and violence, and if you mixed them together, so much the better. The problem was that there
didn't seem to be too many ways to show violence and
still compete with the real thing on the Seven o'clock
News; and sex in films was enmeshed in a controversy
that would go all the way to the Supreme Court. So we
were trapped. I could no longer separate the problems
we were having in film and television from the problems
of the country. Each was caught up in the other. Until
our values as a society improved, our films and television
weren't going to.

I made a decision. With a presidential election coming
up, I wanted to help change things and the best way to
do that was through politics. I didn't want to go into
politics, but I felt I had to. I would work for a candidate
who wasn't afraid to face the truth of what we had become—even if it was painful.

Nine

IN AUGUST 1970, I had thrown a dinner party for George McGovern at my home in California. At the time, McGovern was a blur to most of the people at that party, a man who had made a good impression in a televised debate before the California caucus at the Democratic National Convention in 1968, but who had remained a rather marginal political figure since then. I had been a McGovern delegate to that convention, and decided that a dinner was the best way for some people of wealth and influence to get to know him better. For George McGovern, in 1970, was already running for president.

After dinner, McGovern rose to speak. He was dressed in a neat blue-and-white striped suit that was peculiarly uncreased. In the steady monotone that was later to become so familiar, he raised and answered questions, touching on everything from the role of America as policeman of the world to the legalization of marijuana. He was decent, sincere, a good man. But most of the guests were not impressed.

"This guy's better than Seconal," I heard a guest say. And later, the reports were equally down. No charisma, no pizzazz, no passion, boring, can't pull votes, a loser. It was a typical California response, with emphasis on McGovern as a theatrical act. No one mentioned what he stood for; they only criticized *how* he stood.

McGovern had a small, tight staff; he was preparing

position papers, and he had already formally announced his candidacy. Of all the men running for the right to meet Richard Nixon that year, he struck me as the most decent, the most flexible, the man who might actually be serious about changing the values of the country.

So one afternoon in February 1972, I placed a call to McGovern headquarters in Washington and told them I was ready to start doing everything I could to help get him elected. They called back and told me to take the next plane to New Hampshire.

The snows of New Hampshire were already an American political cliché by the time I found myself there, but those days were among the most exhilarating of my life; ironically, we would refer to them later as the "dark days of the campaign." In the early weeks, before the press started paying attention, McGovern headquarters was the room McGovern slept in at the Howard Johnson Motor Lodge in Manchester. You could see his grandson toddling around with a pacifier in his mouth, or his wife, Eleanor, moving in and out, keeping her own campaign schedule. Field workers dropped in for advice, and the press room was filled with movie stars (Dennis Weaver, Marlo Thomas, Leonard Nimoy, and athlete Ray Schoenke) and potential contributors who were looking McGovern over like booking agents. Nearly everyone campaigning for McGovern was better-known than he was.

I had never been on a campaign trail before. Being a delegate at a convention is an entirely different experience. I found my days beginning at six A.M. with doughnuts and grapeade snatched from a machine in

Howard Johnson's plastic lobby. From there I would visit up to twenty homes a day where I was fed chocolate chip cookies and tarts after speaking about the necessity for change in America. For some reason coconut cakes were a big favorite in the living rooms of strangers at night. It was the hardest battle my waistline ever fought, and the waistline lost. At the end of the campaign, I was twenty-five pounds heavier.

At first I was self-conscious about being a movie star. I knew why I was there: it was to gain attention for the candidate, and to help draw a crowd. I was embarrassed when people asked me questions about Hollywood and why I was doing this. I wasn't running; George Mc-Govern was. But soon people began to respect the simple fact that I took the time to do it at all. There were still the incongruities: discussions of *Irma La Douce* and *The Apartment* and "What is Warren Beatty really like?" but it was soon followed by talk about the military budget, Vietnam, and morality in government. The people I met in New Hampshire and in all the other states where I campaigned were inherently fair; I was a celebrity, yes, but I was also an American, and they respected that. It took a little longer for the press to take me as seriously as the people did. But that wasn't only *my* problem. In a far more important way, George McGovern was suffering from the same thing.

After a few days' work I began to understand that the two most important people in the campaign, after McGovern himself, were an odd couple named Gary Hart and Frank Mankiewicz. I would see Hart, a tall, lean young man of thirty-four, his hair fashionably long, moving around in the lobby, lavishing his attention on the growing army of young workers who were living on peanut butter sandwiches, and who were to be the basis of whatever success McGovern would have.

"Hell, I'm just a country boy," he would say, kicking his boots like Gary Cooper. "I think probably after the primary here, I'll have finished my task for the senator. He'll win a surprisingly large number of votes and then the pols will move in and take over. I can't fight that. So I'll head on back to Colorado."

But I knew the country boy was in it for the duration. He loved reading military history, and admired Napoleon, and there was a military quality to the way he was organizing the young. No he would never give up. All through 1970–71, he had traveled around the country for McGovern, promising a new world to the young, a world that would be free of political hacks, where our latent idealism would be welded to real power. They had listened too, and part of McGovern's success came from the way those young people took over state caucuses, ran state conventions, insisted on a new deal in the picking of delegates to the 1972 convention. Gary was a shrewd cowboy. There were moments late at night when you wanted to rush in and protect him from all the ruthless manipulators he said were around in the world. Not many people realized that he was more attractively manipulative than anyone else.

Frank Mankiewicz was entirely different, yet oddly similar. His mind was a brilliant mix of sophisticated wit, savage humor, and dazzling circuitousness. He had an extraordinary gift for articulating difficult thoughts. He could also be abrasive, self-destructive, and insensitive. In many ways, he was his father's son.

Herman J. Mankiewicz had been a fine screenwriter

(*Citizen Kane, It's a Wonderful World*), a compulsive gambler, a famous drunk, a slashing wit, and a man who was almost ferociously accident prone. Pauline Kael in *The Citizen Kane Book* described him as "a giant of a man who mongered his own talent, a man who got a head start in the race to sell out to Hollywood." Even today, years after his death, the Herman Mankiewicz legend lives on in Hollywood.

As I watched Frank Mankiewicz work in the early stages of the campaign, I remembered a conversation I had had in England with young Tom Mankiewicz. Tom was the son of Herman's brother, the fine director Joseph Mankiewicz, and was creating a career of his own as a screenwriter. I mentioned to Tom that I was thinking of working for George McGovern.

"Be careful, Shirley," he said. "Frank is a wonderful guy, but he will probably self-destruct. All the Mankiewiczes do. I will too, probably. Just when things get going well, he'll shit on it—you watch. He did it with his law practice, he did it with the Peace Corps. Just when his newspaper column started catching on, he did it again. He'll probably do it with George too."

I listened, had a small chill, but soon forgot about our conversation.

We lost the New Hampshire primary, but surprised everyone by finishing a strong second to Edmund Muskie. Muskie should have won by a huge margin. Instead, he had broken down and cried in front of the *Manchester Union-Leader* because that newspaper had made disparaging remarks about his wife, and because it had printed a letter implying that Muskie had racist attitudes toward "Canucks." (The letter, as the country learned after the election, was written by the Nixon campaign's "dirty tricks" department.)

But Muskie was mortally wounded, and would never recover from New Hampshire. Suddenly, George Mc-Govern was a serious candidate.

Ten

MY FIRSTHAND political education was in full swing. After New Hampshire there were palm trees and Coppertone in Florida, dirty snow and factories in Wisconsin, desert and Indians in New Mexico, mountains and pollution in Utah, flat prairies and wind in South Dakota, tacos and beer in Texas, suburban wastelands in New Jersey, and stops in Michigan, Maryland, Vermont, Washington, and many other places that seem a blur to me now. Sometimes I didn't even know where I was. In the primary states, the apparatus of the McGovern campaign was present, full of noise, youth, hope, action, and reporters. In the nonprimary states, campaigning was more lonely. But I was learning. So the exhaustion, the terrible food, and the intermittent feeling of isolation all seemed worth it.

I learned first of all that politics was a form of theater. In Florida, the movie stars came out in force as Lorne Greene of "Bonanza" rode in convertibles with Hubert Humphrey, while Carroll O'Connor did TV spots for John Lindsay and Red Skelton told jokes for Richard Nixon. The candidates were theatrical too. George Wallace would turn his rallies into revival meetings straight out of *Elmer Gantry*. John Lindsay jumped into the ocean off the Florida Keys in a bathing suit, to display his concern about pollution, and looked as if he were trying to revive "Sea Hunt." We weren't certain what McGovern's theatrical style was; it was probably the absence of style altogether.

I also learned that one of the high priorities in any campaign is fund raising, and with McGovern it came a dollar at a time. Night after night I would attend fund-raising cocktail parties, where, as the star attraction, I was expected to be not only charming, but so well-informed about the life and record of George McGovern that I would electrify the freeloaders in the audience into springing for a grand a drink. Sometimes it actually happened.

Usually I promised to go to Acapulco with anyone who would give $5,000 to the campaign, explaining that such a sum would buy two weeks of peanut butter for McGovern's young army. I hoped Gloria Steinem wouldn't hear about that approach. Other times, Pierre Salinger and I would team up, with him playing a great fraternity house piano while I sang parodies and danced. Pierre and I traveled all over the country, usually on airplanes that seemed left over from some old John Wayne movie, and one night I was so tired I fell asleep leaning against a pillar on someone's porch.

But it was the people who were crucial, and as I moved among them, I learned that America was a kaleidoscope.

In Northeast Philadelphia, I was greeted at the door by a harried mother of four, whose dark orange lipstick and hair in curlers seemed to signal a fantasy that her life would change soon. She was carrying a box of cereal and her wedding picture adorned the top of the TV set that was blaring in the background. I could see a picture of Jesus Christ on the wall. The place smelled of babies as her four children sat staring at a TV game show, their clothes strewn on the floor.

"Hi there, honey," she said. "Come on in if you want.

We're so poor it doesn't matter what happens in the election. The rich people do what they want anyway, so we don't vote in this place. But sit down."

She didn't think candidate Chisholm would make a good president because "he's not man enough for the job." She didn't know whether Chisholm was a hawk or a dove, "but I read somewhere that hawks eat babies, so I guess I'd be a dove. I don't like the Communists, I know that."

She said she knew nothing about politics and was just glad her husband had a job at Nabisco. Women's liberation was OK with her, "as long as they didn't go too far." When I left she asked me if I thought voting really made any difference.

In Michigan I heard a young man argue *for* George Wallace against an *old* man who thought Wallace was dangerous. A college group I addressed in Illinois talked cynically among themselves, showing by their rudeness that they thought nothing good could happen within the system, but another group in Colorado raised the roof in enthusiasm when I brought up the same issues.

In Massachusetts, I was met by a couple campaigning for McGovern with a yellow Rolls-Royce and champagne in an ice bucket. In New York I visited McGovern storefronts in the most desperate slums. Accents changed, styles were different, customs and even cultural habits altered from state to state. I found that there were a dozen, perhaps twenty different Americas out there.

I shared dinners with people all over the country, and sometimes they would call themselves "The Randolphs" or "The Johnsons." The wives seldom had first names; they were extensions of their husbands. The middle-class families were an important part of the McGovern

constituency; yet they often seemed rather rigid, react-
ing with status-conscious fears as they supervised their
children who were seen but not heard (at least in the
presence of strangers). It was in these living rooms that
the future of America would be settled.

Sometimes I campaigned along with McGovern as he
shook hands at the gates of factories, ate platefuls of
lasagna and spaghetti, gave civics lessons at high schools
where the seniors were eligible to vote, met with labor
leaders, spoke in churches, rode miles through icy rain
and snow, signed autographs in local bars, and always
emphasized the need for change in America.

I made some real mistakes. Once in Pittsburgh, I
spoke to a black women's luncheon, which followed a
fashion show. The women sat at long tables with plastic
plates of fried chicken before them, along with Dixie
cups of apple juice. As I talked I watched their hats,
decorated with fruit and flowers, bobbing gently. I developed my thesis about how things were going to get
better. How they as black women represented a sector
of America that had had nothing long enough. How we
were coming into a time when everyone would realize
that America had cared too much for too long about
the wrong things. When I finished, the response was
polite silence. I didn't understand.

"You can't tell those women that stuff," a young
black man said afterward. "You can't tell them they
don't have much. They're proud people, and many of
them want the things—those very things—that you
think are useless."

This was in the same country where a man in Green
Bay, Wisconsin, told me: "If you live in Green Bay and
you're black, you'd better be a Green Bay Packer."

Meantime, I got to know a lot of the American press. At least that part of the American press that travels with political candidates. I loved the times when I would come back from the boondocks, and return to the center of the primary state action. I would sit up through the night with the journalists, listening to their abrasive jokes, watching them operate with a half quart of Scotch in them, as they also admitted that they didn't know what the hell was going on in America.

They sensed that McGovern's growing success indicated a silent revolution might be taking place in America. But they also knew that things changed rapidly in America, and they had learned to distrust what was true today because it might not be true tomorrow. They respected accuracy, worshiped hard facts, and ironically that seemed to limit their overall accuracy.

Theodore White thought it was "cute" that anyone could believe McGovern would win the nomination, a position he changed after the Wisconsin primary. Doug Kiker of CBS told me that in 1968 George Wallace had asked him to be his running mate. I didn't know whether to believe him or not. The line between truth and fiction was rapidly narrowing.

"Being a confirmed cynic," NBC's John Chancellor would say, "I find you enchanting. How about a martini?"

In all the bars in the big hotels in the primary states, the new arrivals, travel-strained and weary, would come in for gin and comfort, and tell the others what they were picking up. They would carefully pry me for "inside information" about the McGovern campaign, filing away personal tidbits, which would turn up weeks later in some obscure paragraph of a story. Every night you

would see a chosen member of the McGovern staff
dining with a chosen member of the press, and it was
difficult to decide who was using whom.

I came to admire the skepticism of the press, and
their suspiciousness, realizing that in the last analysis
their job was to tell the public as much of the truth as
they could get their hands on. They were limited, of
course, by the amount of available space in their newspapers, or time in their news shows. And when they were
finished working, they played as hard as any of the
people I had known in the lush days in Hollywood. But
they were honest men.

A lot of them had a knack for appearing anonymous.
In many cases, they didn't just blend into the woodwork,
they *were* the woodwork, being absorbed into elevators,
restaurants, and hallways as though they were tourists.
You could always tell the TV reporters from the radio
and print reporters. The TV men watched their weight,
ate lots of salads, skipped the potatoes, dressed meticu-
lously, and were constantly aware of their own facial
movements and the way they came across in a conversation. The print reporters lived for words. They would
remember the precise way McGovern had said something, or would force me to be more precise when I went
off on one of my airier flights of rhetoric. They remembered lead paragraphs from stories written in 1926, and
seemed to be walking file cabinets of information.

There was an accepted hierarchy in the press corps,
too, although none of them would have admitted it.
The man from the *New York Times* was the star in press
situations, followed by the man from the *Washington
Post*. The competition was fierce, and the politicians
—even McGovern's mixed bag of amateurs and old

pros—knew how to play the press perfectly. All of them felt they should be near the center of the action, and it wasn't until later that we learned where the real center of the action was. In the aftermath of a burglary at the Watergate Apartments in Washington, two police reporters named Woodward and Bernstein had the biggest story of the decade.

Probably the grandest media star of all was Walter Cronkite. When he walked in, the bar usually stopped cold. He was the Dean, the man the polls had described as "the most trusted man in America." He was personally a warm, stable, soothing man, with surprising modesty, but what I remember best about him was a night in Florida when he walked into the Four Ambassadors, nodded hello as he passed along the row of profiles at the bar, and then saw a large picture hat lying by itself on the bar.

"Oh my God," he said, "Bella Abzug fell off her stool."

We won Wisconsin, and with that first victory everything seemed to change. In the hotel lobby people were talking in hushed tones, as if they were expecting the arrival of the pope. The Secret Service men were around now, with walkie-talkies and crewcuts. It was impossible now to walk casually into McGovern's room, see his grandson toddling around, and talk politics, and the change in atmosphere wasn't good for McGovern. He was already too guarded and private a man, and a wall of Secret Service men would not make him more open. He needed advice and criticism on a direct basis, not by way of memos and crowded meetings.

In the coffee shop the next morning, Theodore H.

White took my arm and said, "Well, kid, *now* this race is a great story." He was right, even if some of us thought it had taken him a long time to see it.

I moved on then, into Pennsylvania and Massachusetts, listening as best I could to America, feeling increasingly lonely. I was sleeping in a different hotel room every night, meeting only strangers, never having time to make friends or learn anything real about those I did meet. I was meeting thousands of people and getting to know none of them.

Late one night, I sat at the hotel window, looking out at a city and suddenly I realized I couldn't remember which city it was. I wondered why I was doing all this. I had turned down three pictures, something I couldn't afford to do after the debacle of the TV series. But I had made a commitment to myself, and my voyage through America had only deepened it. Everywhere I went, Americans were angry or suspicious or fearful or violent or poor or simply numb. It was hard to think of ways to make them laugh, and the more I learned about them the more I felt my own sense of humor dwindling. My friends, my work, my "money-making potential"—my life, really—were on the back burner. The personal price I was paying was very high. But there didn't seem to be any important movies to make anyway because there was nothing much to feel good about.

There was fun in the campaigning, real fun. But I could sense, more than ever before, that if changes weren't made soon in the way America felt about itself and its leaders, it was going to be too late. For movies. For fun. For almost anything human.

Eleven

I DIDN'T REALIZE IT then, but for me Wisconsin was the high point in McGovern's run for the presidency. It wasn't only because of his subsequent mistakes. It was because the more I became involved in "big time" politics the more I realized how vicious the in-fighting could get in the desire to "make things better."

Still speaking, fund-raising, eating, informing, listening, persuading, laughing, and learning, I moved on to California. I campaigned at barbecues, coffee klatches, churches, high schools, bowling alleys, beer halls, and colleges. Some people seemed to care—others no longer believed that anything or anyone could make a difference in what had gone wrong in their lives. The college campuses seemed golden green and creamy to me as the students lolled in the grass when McGovern spoke. Sometimes he aroused them to passion. More often than not I couldn't tell *what* they were thinking. Mexican-Americans hung piñatas in trees to greet us and the blacks were warm and friendly, remembering McGovern's voting record in the Senate, but no one was truly electrified.

We were in California and McGovern was not Bobbie Kennedy, and no one knew that better than McGovern himself. California was the "snake pit"—the big one, and the most unpredictable state in the union. With the pressure of such an important primary building, I sat back and watched. I could feel a shift within the campaign staff. I wasn't politically sophisticated enough to know the details of what was going on—I only knew, after years in Hollywood, that large grabs for power were in the works. I thought McGovern would stand monolithically at the top, orchestrating his staff. But he didn't. He seemed to be unable to make himself clear on what he would tolerate and what he wouldn't. I would sit in the coffee shop of the Wilshire Hyatt House talking to Mankiewicz and Hart and realize that McGovern had told them something entirely different from what he had told me. I wondered if he was doing it on purpose. He would express his anger and disapproval, but never address the person in question directly. He apparently believed in a democratically run campaign, but I was beginning to wonder if that was simply because he didn't know how to be a decisive leader. He said he wanted an open campaign, but it was becoming more and more closed. At the end of the day he tended to isolate himself with members of his staff or a sheaf of memos. Always a shy man, he preferred to ruminate alone rather than allow people to come and go freely in his hotel room. He didn't like talking on the phone, whether it was to contact people for money or just to see how they were feeling. He seemed reluctant to expose his basic feelings, and I thought often of what Bill Dougherty, lieutenant governor of South Dakota and the man who knew McGovern best, had said about him; "Inside George McGovern," he said, "lies an inscrutable Chinese man. You never really know what he's thinking."

I reflected often on my reasons for being for McGovern in the first place. I felt I knew him fairly well

—enough to work hard for him—but there were things now that began to bother me. He wasn't comfortable with ethnic Americans, feeling either threatened by or detached from their individual cultures. For instance he insisted, even after a waitress warned him not to, on having milk with chopped chicken liver in a Jewish delicatessen. He never knew how to act with Mexicans or Puerto Ricans or Italians or wild Irish intellectuals. He seemed uncomfortable with people who were overt or aggressive.

What bothered me most was how uncomfortable he felt with women. And what bothered *him* most was how women felt about *abortion*.

I had had an unsatisfactory discussion with him about abortion right after the Massachusetts primary. I hadn't been able to understand what his position was in our private talk, much less comprehend what he was saying publicly. He saw no contradiction in stating simultaneously that abortion was a state's rights issue, but that a woman and her doctor should be allowed to make the decision. Then he said he would stand behind the pending Supreme Court decision. If the decision was negative he said he would cross that bridge when he came to it. I told him, as had many of the leaders of the women's movement, that the progressive women of America, who were his natural constituency, expected him to defend their right to exercise control over their own bodies. McGovern didn't agree. He either personally believed, or was being influenced by people who personally believed, that after ten weeks or so a woman had no right to decide whether or not she would terminate a pregnancy. I was stunned. I tried to convince him that you are either in favor of a woman's right to make the decision or you're not. It was not a *question* of *when* or for how long she had the right. When he referred to the large Catholic population whom he might be offending not *politically* but *personally,* I knew abortion was an issue too explosive for him to handle. He wasn't sure how he felt about it. I was worried about what would happen when the public realized this.

So I made a decision which was something I'd have to live with from then on. It was better for McGovern not to face the issue *at all*—particularly in the face of the distortion he could expect from Richard Nixon. I waited, expecting a program or position paper to evolve. Nothing happened. In the Midwestern primary states, Humphrey and Jackson had picked up McGovern's inconsistency on abortion (as well as on marijuana, which he thought should be decriminalized but not legalized). Because McGovern was not clear in his own mind he couldn't respond decisively to their accusations. So he ended up being labeled radical about something he didn't believe in. The women's movement was getting more and more confused as to McGovern's real beliefs and the subject of abortion became a hot potato.

None of the other women on the campaign staff seemed concerned. They were more involved with delegate strength, logistics, and fund raising. That left me. So McGovern and I had another discussion and he asked me to take charge of "the problem." What that meant was that as a delegate from California serving on the platform committee I was to try to keep abortion *off* the majority plank.

For the next few weeks I found myself fighting against something I believed in strongly because the important thing was to elect George McGovern.

I began to have serious doubts that it was worth working so hard for the betterment of a society in which this was the price. The means were somehow getting confused with the end. I wasn't sure either was justified.

The political ruthlessness was shocking too. I remember the evpression on McGovern's face when, after winning the California, winner-take-all, primary, he was arbitrarily challenged by his old friend Hubert Humphrey. It wasn't the challenge itself that got McGovern. It was "the hate and vehemence in Hubert's eyes," he said.

I was bewildered by a system that tolerated such destructive acts of political competition. There was no way Humphrey could make his winner-take-all challenge beneficial to himself. It was only a stop-McGovern move, and its arbitrary sense of ruthless defiance was astonishing.

But then I remember sitting alone in my hotel room, with the mascara running under my eyes as McGovern stepped from the California podium after his victory. It was June 5 and I wondered if there was a kitchen behind him. I wondered where Dutton and Mankiewicz and Salinger were. I was just thankful that McGovern, with all the weaknesses of his campaign, had made it through California alive.

Twelve

IT'S STRANGE now, after everything that's happened, to recall convention week in Miami. It was my second convention as a delegate and after the debacle of Chicago this seemed the year that hope might actually have a chance. Even though some of us in the campaign had already become aware that our Knight on a White Charger was a man after all, we felt good about his making participatory democracy work. The delegates were more representative than at any previous convention, thanks to McGovern reform rules.

It seems ironic now, but then we really believed through the democratic process that we could force a peaceful end to the Vietnam war, reverse the trend of military spending, begin to clean up the cities, and in general get down to the business of what America was supposed to be about. I remember feeling so often that this was probably our last chance. I don't know why that thought stuck in my mind, but I had some growing heavy feeling that without McGovern (as preposterous as his election seemed), it would all be too late.

Miami was a hot blast in the face, a shimmering place full of pink and white architecture, turquoise pools, and palm trees. It was more like a magical stage set than a real city. I moved through a world of hotels that week, great baroque palaces filled with luggage, bellhops, delegates, cables, arguments, angry blacks, angry women, the angry and often arrogant young, and the candidates themselves.

Mornings ran into afternoons in a sun-blazed rush; there were midnight meetings and caucuses at dawn, drinks across the evenings, and lunches with people whose votes were often more important than those of the famous people who were trying to change them. There were fights over credentials, especially in my delegation from California, with the Humphrey people trying to ruin McGovern's victory by insisting that the winner-take-all concept was against the convention rules. The Humphrey people had run with those rules all through the primary and only wanted to change the rules now that the ball game was over. The arguments were tedious and complicated; but everybody knew that Humphrey had no real chance of winning the nomination. Humphrey's only motivation was to prevent McGovern from winning it. Such was the self-destruction of the Democrat. It seems irrelevant now, but in those frantic days, while some speakers took the stand to denounce homosexuals as child molesters, and Jesse Jackson denounced Mayor Daley like a conquering hero (only to sell out to the Nixon people later in the campaign), it seemed as if America really would stand or fall on what happened in that red-carpeted big convention hall in that theatrical Disneyland of a city.

At 4:00 A.M. on the third day of the convention, Section Number 7 on rights, power, and social justice came before the convention, and I could feel the butterflies in my stomach. The abortion fight was about to begin. At the platform committee hearings a few weeks earlier, I had successfully maneuvered to keep abortion off the

majority plank. Even though it was a crucial issue to
women, I had asked that McGovern not be compelled to
run on an issue where he could be badly hurt by the
Nixon forces. I wanted the women to compromise, to
get McGovern elected first, and then, from a position
of power, and with a debt to collect, change the abortion
laws.

But I was soon caught between the rock and the hard
place. The leaders of the women's movement could never
be sure whether I was working for women or for Mc-
Govern. The McGovern people were having the same
problem. Later Gloria Steinem would write that I had a
case of "campaignitis," because I stood for compromise.

In any case, I drained five glasses of orange juice back-
stage, and then mounted the podium, to stare into
10,000 faces. As I spoke I urged everyone present to vote
his or her own conscience on the issue of abortion. I said
that every woman had a right to control her own body,
that one day the fight would be won, but that for now, I
thought it would be better to keep the issue out of the
arena of presidential politics. Otherwise, Nixon and his
people would hurt both the candidate *and* the issue.

A confused cheer went up. The delegates had the
right to be confused. When I went back to the California delegation to wait for the vote, Walter Cronkite
called me from his glass booth and asked me how I
voted. I told him that since I had asked the delegates to
vote their consciences, I had done the same thing, and
my conscience told me to vote *for* an abortion plank,
even though I had suggested that in the interests of victory the delegates should vote *against* it. Walter seemed
properly confused.

Then Willie Brown, a California assemblyman from

San Francisco who was leading our delegation, reported that the Humphrey-Wallace forces were teaming up to vote *for* abortion, as a means of embarrassing McGovern. "Those sons of bitches," Willie shouted. "We went along with a legitimate vote of conscience. If that's how they're gonna play, I'll cast all 271 votes from California against it!"

When the women heard this, they jumped on Willie in a fury, but he had no time to respond. Pierre Salinger rushed up, reporting that North Carolina was going big for abortion. The fix was in. "Now we have to do something." So the word went to the floor from the McGovern control center: lobby, arm twist, plead: anything to keep abortion off the platform, Stunned, I stood by the red telephone.

I saw the imposing form of Bella Abzug moving from delegation to delegation, asking for a "yes" vote, "because it would lose anyway." I could see Gloria Steinem having a wild argument with Joe Duffey, a McGovern floor manager, because he had allowed someone to speak for the rights of the fetus, something Joe said he had not done. It was confusion, nearing hysteria, and then someone noticed that abortion was losing. Salinger's information was wrong; North Carolina was not going with abortion to embarrass McGovern. In fact, the women's caucus from that state, led by a decidedly nontheatrical woman from Greensboro named Martha McKay, had convinced the men in the delegation to vote according to their consciences, which is what I had urged them to do.

The minority plank—which would have forced McGovern to run with abortion as an issue—lost. We adjourned at 6:20 in the morning. The press had largely vanished. The galleries were empty. In the glass booths above the delegates, the TV anchor men were telling anybody who was still awake, or just rising, that they admired our patience, discipline, and diligence.

I went back to the hotel, and George McGovern called me. He thanked me for what I had done. He said he knew how much my action had cost me in terms of principle and understood how difficult it must have been for me to put political necessity over personal conviction. He then asked me if I would put together a women's arm for the national campaign, because he could not be elected without the women's vote. I said yes. Afterward, I went down to the ocean and took a swim.

Two days later, at two in the morning, George McGovern accepted the nomination of the Democratic party. Edward Kennedy had made an electrifying speech, and now stood beside McGovern, smiling for the cameras and what was left of the TV audience. To McGovern's right, also smiling, and sweating in what we thought was the heat from the lights, was the man who would be McGovern's vice presidential running mate, Senator Tom Eagleton from Missouri. He looked like a nice man.

Thirteen

I WENT TO the Hamptons to rest from the convention, to soak up the sea, to start planning the women's arm in a campaign dominated by men. I walked along the sand, listened to the pounding of the surf, and did a lot of thinking. Then one morning, the phone rang. It was Jimmy Breslin.

"It's all fuckin' over," he said.

"What's over, Jimmy? You've thought it's been over for a long time."

"No," he said. "This time it's fuckin' true."

"What do you mean?"

"Shock treatment," he said flatly.

"What are you talking about?"

"The fuckin' bastard had shock treatment." His voice was rising now.

"Who had shock treatment?"

"Eagleton. The fuckin' vice president will have to be plugged in if he travels. If the city blacks out, we'll know it's our guy gettin' a fix. It's fuckin' all over. Good-by."

He hung up. I turned on the radio. It was true. Eagleton and McGovern had called a press conference to discuss Eagleton's medical history, after a newspaper report that Eagleton had been hospitalized at least three times for depression and had received shock therapy. I called Gary Hart in Washington.

"Gary," I said, "what's all this about Eagleton?"

"All what?" he asked lazily.

"The shock treatment."

"Oh, that."

He didn't seem concerned. As I think about it now, it's clear to me that the casualness was crucial to the dénouement of the campaign. I explained to Gary that Eagleton must have been very disturbed to have required shock therapy. But that wasn't the issue. The important thing was that Eagleton had lied to McGovern, and for that reason alone he should be kicked off the ticket.

Gary told me that it would "blow over," and that I shouldn't worry so much. I hung up. I called Fred Dutton in South Dakota. He, too, was unconcerned.

"New York's not the center of the world, you know," he said. "Out here it's on the eighth page of the *Denver Post*, and that's where it'll stay."

That was it. What happened is familiar to everyone. The nation watched as McGovern said he backed Eagleton a thousand percent, and then spent six days trying to get him off the ticket. McGovern's inconsistency was glaringly revealed, as well as his apparent weakness under pressure. I knew that McGovern's innate decency was struggling with the political practicalities, and that whatever happened, his credibility would lose. It did, and that was the election.

At one point I started talking about the possibilities of having Eagleton replaced by Cissy Farenthold from Texas. She had finished second to Eagleton in the number of votes at the convention, and she was a strong, fresh candidate who might attract a lot of women to the damaged candidacy of McGovern. I mentioned this to a young McGovern fund raiser named Bill Rosendahl, who apparently telephoned McGovern. McGovern was furious and demanded that I call him. As we talked I could hear family sounds in the background.

"I understand you're upset," I said.

His voice was cold and decisive. "I'm not upset," he said. "I'm outraged. How dare you do such a thing without my instructions?"

I told him I wasn't mounting a campaign for Cissy, I was checking the idea with people who wanted McGovern to beat Richard Nixon. I told him that he, McGovern, had sent word out, in various ways, that he was dumping Eagleton, and wanted other suggestions. Cissy Farenthold was my suggestion. He listened as I outlined my reasons for believing a Farenthold candidacy would work. When I finished, he apologized. He told me not to worry; he wouldn't offer the job to Hubert Humphrey or any other tired politician—but particularly Humphrey.

"I give you my word I won't ask him," he said. "As a matter of fact, I was offered over a million dollars if I'd take him, but I refused. So don't be concerned about him."

Then he talked about Eagleton.

"He's a real bastard," McGovern said. "You have no idea. I think there's a chance he might have withdrawn on his own. But after Jack Anderson accused him of drunken driving, he dug in deeper. He's a real son of a bitch, and it makes me angry even to discuss him."

Two days later, Eagleton was gone, and McGovern offered the vice presidency to Hubert Humphrey.

The rest of the campaign was a holding operation. The candidacy was mortally wounded. Sargent Shriver finally replaced Eagleton, and McGovern started to run against Nixon. He made a lot of small mistakes, and although all of them combined didn't compare to a single day in the criminal record of Nixon's administration, they projected the image of McGovern as a weak, unsure man who was somehow out of his league. Since Nixon wouldn't run in the open, wrapping himself instead in the security of the presidency, the reporters had no Nixon to observe and criticize. McGovern was the only visible candidate.

Slowly people began to desert the campaign. The professional Democratic politicians wanted to disassociate themselves from the presidential campaign and do whatever they could to survive a Nixon landslide. Some of the celebrities and movie stars who had backed McGovern were suddenly busy making movies or being celebrities. I continued to travel the country, but campaigning had become a drudgery, as I was always in the position of defending McGovern, instead of celebrating him as a bright alternative to Nixon. There was something about the fact that McGovern's humiliations had taken place in *public* that made him an embarrassment to so many people. It was clear that the electorate really didn't want "open" politics, if being "open" meant letting your mistakes hang out there for the world to see.

I traveled to twenty more states. The American conscience seemed numb. The people simply didn't care that McGovern had not bombed Cambodia, made deals with ITT, or engineered a disastrous wheat deal with the Soviets from which his friends all profited. It wasn't McGovern who was laundering secret campaign money in Mexico, impounding funds, vetoing day care centers, or raising milk price supports in exchange for campaign contributions. Nor did McGovern send burglars out to wiretap and rob the opposition party. After a long day's campaigning, I would watch the news on TV and see McGovern's wounded face as he tried to struggle on, and sometimes I would just sit there and cry.

On election night, we were all in a small suite at the Holiday Inn in Sioux Falls, South Dakota. The room was quiet and hushed as the numbers piled up and defeat was recorded on the TV set. Sheddings from the thick green carpet clung to the backs of our shoes, as I watched the fat cats file into the living room. There was no ice left in the bucket. The pretzels were gone, and there were two bottles of Seven-Up, and a bottle each of Scotch, vodka, and gin on top of the TV set. Somehow it reminded me of the poverty of those small living rooms in New Hampshire where it had all started.

Then McGovern came in, towering above most of the people in the room, accompanied by a lone Secret Service man with a hearing device plugged into his ear. They never shoot losers in America, so McGovern had nothing to fear. The exhausted droop of the last weeks of the campaign was gone, and now McGovern looked like a man bending gracefully with the wind. Being back in South Dakota probably had something to do with it. He was home, and there he had nobility in defeat.

His skin was mellow and tawny from a hundred outdoor rallies and as I looked at him his face registered conflict, as if he was trying to make up his mind whether to preach for a living or stand up and shout at the preacher. He moved slowly around the room, shaking hands and thanking everyone, talking of past experiences, hard work, the need to keep faith, asking people about their lives and families and futures.

He stopped in front of me. I looked into his eyes. They

didn't waver. He wrapped his arms around me—then pulled away and put out his hand. His handshake was firm and solid. "Thanks, pal," he said. "You were there from the beginning and you're here at the end." I took a deep breath.

I wanted to tell him how much I admired him, how much he had meant to all of us, how little the mistakes really mattered when you measured them against the crimes of the people in power, and how important it was that, for a few brief moments, decency seemed to live in the world again.

But I never got to say any of that. Eleanor McGovern grabbed me and sobbed into my hair. "We'll never do anything like this again," she said. I patted her on the back, remembering a friend of mine whose marriage had collapsed because he came home to his wife every night, filled with pain and problems and worry, and she would pat him on the back. "Those goddamned sympathetic pats," he said. "What were they supposed to mean? All I wanted was some meat and potatoes."

And then, as quietly as he had appeared, McGovern was gone. It was over. I reached for the can of mixed nuts, but it was empty.

In the morning I woke to a daytime television show on which women were competing for waffle irons and trips to Bermuda. I went downstairs, where McGovern was walking through the last group of supporters, shaking hands, saying good-by, and I followed him as he walked to a Cadillac, long and black and powerful, to meet Eleanor, who was holding an armful of red roses. A light rain was falling, and the car pulled slowly away, then gradually picked up speed until it was out of sight.

I looked up at the storm clouds, and saw the sign of the Holiday Inn. The night before it had said: "Welcome Home, Senator." Now the sign of welcome was gone, replaced by a simpler message: "It's over."

Fourteen

TWO MONTHS LATER, I went to Washington to see the second inauguration of Richard Milhous Nixon. I had never been to an inauguration before, but I wanted to see this one: to see what happens after a year like 1972 ends, to look at the faces of the people who were going to run America for four more years. I bought a ticket and sat with thousands of Republican party faithful on wooden stands facing the White House. My feet froze and my spirit was colder, as the affair—which was organized by someone named Jeb Stuart Magruder—evolved before me. It was a wild, boastful military display, filled with marching bands and men in costumes straight out of the Austro-Hungarian Empire. It was like a halftime show at the Super Bowl, but with real weapons. Nixon sat behind the bullet-proof glass of his reviewing stand across the street with all the president's men around him. The big cover-up was already in full swing, although we didn't know it then.

When I had had enough, and while the marching bands were still blasting away with songs of patriotism and war, I left my place, went to a phone booth, and called my parents, who lived across the river in Arlington.

"Where are you, Shirl?" my dad said. "We were looking for you on television at the Washington Monument. Lots of those hippie protestors making damn fools of themselves. We were relieved 'cause you weren't there, and then we saw that yellow sound truck comin' around a corner with somebody making a damn fool shrill speech. And we thought, Christ, that might be her. But it wasn't." He seemed relieved. "What happened?"

I told him I had watched the parade, sitting directly across the street from Richard Nixon. There was a puzzled silence on the other end of the line.

"Well, now," Dad said, "I see you finally got smart."

I rented a car and drove over to see my parents. They had moved from one section of Arlington to another since I had last seen them, easing up the economic ladder as so many Americans have. They lived in a *home* now, not a *house*, on a quiet well-kept block where Chevrolet Impalas stood in the driveways. The house was not much different from the old one where my brother, Warren, and I had grown up, except that there were a few more trees now, an extra bedroom, more space between the houses, and, of course, fences. As I pulled up, I saw a paper boy drive by on a bike, looking like something out of an old *Saturday Evening Post*, but I wondered what his sisters were like and whether his older brothers or his father had served in Vietnam. So much was gone now that once seemed permanent.

The front lawn was a brownish yellow on that winter day and I remembered Dad telling me on the telephone that there was a new chemical paint that would make the lawn a permanent green, just the way we did it in the movies. The garden looked skeletal, and I remembered also that Dad had told me my mother was working too hard in the yard.

"What can you do with some women?" he had protested. "My mother was the same way. In fact, your mother's getting to be right much like my mother, in her old age. Couldn't tell either one what was good for 'em."

Mother answered the door in a pair of striped slacks, a checked blouse, a sleeveless vest of quilts, and a bow ribbon clutched around her hair, which was styled in a short cropped pony tail.

"Oh, Shirl," she said, "we're so glad to see you. We were so happy you didn't do anything foolish today."

"Can I go to the bathroom please?" I asked, half meaning it and half wanting to change the subject.

My Bathroom, as they called it because it was next to My Bedroom, was pink. Pink was for girls. The toilet paper was pink, the bathmat was pink, the shower curtain, towels, and Kleenex—pink. Everything matched, the way things always matched in the magazine ads. The shelves were neatly arranged and the pink curtains hung sweetly over cream-colored Venetian blinds. It was lovely.

My Bedroom looked almost exactly like the bedroom I had grown up in: it was, in fact, the same bed, soft and downy deep. The dresser was the same one in front of which I used to brush my hair at night, wondering if I'd ever be pretty enough to satisfy one man for life the way Mother and everyone else was trying to do.

The pictures of sailing ships and flowers and a beautiful, regal woman had been painted by Mother herself. She had been an art student once and loved beauty so much it sometimes made her cry.

I opened the sliding closet doors. Inside were Mother's clothes, hung neatly in a row, and I saw the dresses and shoes I had sent her from Hong Kong. She cherished the things I sent her from my travels; they were a part of me, in some way, telling her that I hadn't gone away from her forever.

She was smiling at me when I turned.

"Is it like you remembered it?" she asked. I told her I had gone through so much this past year that I felt I had come full circle.

"I guess I have, too," she said. "With your daddy turning seventy yesterday and the same thing happening to me soon, we probably don't have much more time. You look around, Shirl, and tell me what things you'd like when we're gone. I'm afraid I might go before you come back here again."

She had never seemed able to face reality, and to hear her talking this way out of necessity was somehow shocking.

"Tomorrow," she said, "you'll see our white pigeons. They come around all the time and they're always together. They never leave each other. They're beautiful."

We walked into the living room together.

"Hi, Monkey," Dad said, lumbering toward me with his arms outstretched, looking dapper and slimmer than I remembered, dressed in a plaid sports jacket. He offered his cheek for me to kiss, but made no contact with his own lips. He seemed shorter somehow and I wondered if people really did shrink with age.

"You lookin' right pretty—here let me look at you," he said, stepping back to suggest that I do a fashion-show twirl. "Yep—right pretty. Now look at this!" He took the waistband of his trousers and shook it away from his body, leaving about two inches of space.

"My God," I said, "you're downright skinny, aren't you?" I remembered how he used to love cold milk spiked with vanilla and a hunk of seven-layer chocolate cake before he went to bed. Everything he ate looked delicious to me then, even the pea soup, which I hated until he gave me a spoonful of his.

"Well, now, let's sit down," said Mother, "and catch up on all the news."

I walked through the living room, decorated with all the old familiar things; antique chairs of lipstick red upholstery, and antique crystal ashtrays that were as unused as the fireplace. The room was not a favorite of theirs; it was a small museum where they could display the collection of a lifetime.

The "sun room" was where they lived. It was all windows with rattan furniture of flowered upholstery. A tall banana plant stood behind Dad's favorite rocking chair and Mother's plants were on all the windowsills.

"The plants are much better when I talk to them," she said. "They need love and affection just like any living thing—aren't they beautiful?"

They were. Healthy and shining, they obviously had become her new children.

"I can feel if they are depressed or in need of something," Mother said, "and after talking to them in soothing tones they're much better."

"I wish your mother felt that way about me," Dad said.

There was a long silence. Then Mother got up to go to the kitchen.

"Well, what have you been up to?" I asked Dad.

"Jury duty," he said. "My first time. Have you ever been called to do that?"

I shook my head no.

"Well, it's right nice to work with these people. Very proper, well-mannered, and sensible people."

He got up from his chair. "Let me show you something, while your mother isn't looking. She doesn't like anybody to know."

He led me into the big back bedroom, opened a

drawer, and proudly displayed four pairs of well-tailored slacks and two plaid sports jackets.

"On sale. Slacks marked down from $39.95 to $20.00 and jackets from $30.00 We had to get them because they were a bargain. I have to look nice, you know, going in for jury duty. Everyone's so well dressed. But your mother tells people we got them at Garfinkels, you know, and she hemmed the cuffs right quick so nobody would see we bought them off the rack." He held the clothes to his body and admired himself.

"We have such beautiful things, Monkey, all those things you send us from all over the world. We are fortunate people."

He looked around the room. "So you decide what things you want to be yours when we die. I know how mean those arguments can be if it's not stipulated in the will."

I thought about my mother out in the kitchen; her cooking had always been tentative, as if somewhere inside she was silently protesting against having to cook. And I thought that if there was anything at all I wanted, it was the blue and yellow cookie jar. That jar was always stacked with cookies that I knew she had *enjoyed* baking, even though I was never sure how she felt about the rest of the job.

"Daddy," I said, "I don't want to hurt your feelings, but I don't care that much."

"Ahhh—you don't now but you will. When the time comes."

"Well, I don't think so. But if you really want me to pick something, I'll pick the cookie jar in the kitchen. Or the dressing table in my bedroom. I had many thoughts sitting at the table, night after night."

"You mean the mirror sitting on the base table?"

"Yes."

"But that's only worth $2.95. I remember when we went down and bought it when we thought you were old enough."

"Well, that's something important, to me."

"OK. Whatever you say."

He led me around the house evaluating each table, chair, picture, and vase. He described the life and origin of each item with an almost religious intensity, appreciating the work and love and labor that went into the production of each of them. I led him back to the living room, and asked him how he felt about jury duty.

"Well," he said, "I sure as hell don't like the responsibility of deciding how long somebody should be sent to the penitentiary."

"Do most of the cases revolve around dope?"

"Shit, yes," he said. "And I feel so sorry for those poor niggers over in Niggertown."

I suggested that maybe they shouldn't go to jail for dope at all since most of the pushers were addicts themselves, trying to support their own habits. Dad's reply surprised me.

"Yeah, I've thought a lot about this," he said. "Maybe it should all be legal. I remember during prohibition, it was the guys who could get the stuff that became the big wheels and the ones who couldn't were nobody. So you drank to be better than anybody else. That made you popular. I probably wouldn't have drunk so much later on if I hadn't thought it was something so special then. You know, before they swear you in for duty they ask if you've got any preconceived ideas about the legalization of dope. Shit—that was a hard one for me. How can you not think about it?"

He lit his pipe, crushing the tobacco in the bowl with surgical precision.

"I don't see," he said quietly, "why you denigrate me for wanting to leave you and Warren nice things. I just want to be sure you're provided for."

I didn't want to hurt him, and as he sat there I told him about a man I had recently met in Texas.

He had worked hard all his life, putting in overtime at the plant whenever he could get it, and I had asked him what he would do if he suddenly found he had six months to live and his family asked him to quit work and stay home with them. He said he wouldn't stay home. His responsibilities as a father and head of the house demanded that he leave his family as much money as he could accumulate in the time he had left. He said nothing was more important than providing for them, even if *they* wanted *him* more than money. "I didn't argue with him, Daddy," I said, "because that's what he believed in. But as far as I'm concerned, I think he cared about the wrong thing."

"OK, children," said Mother. "Dinner's on the table, such as it is."

The table was set with family heirlooms: crystal glasses left to my mother by her mother, lace place mats —symbols of gentility—silver that I had loved to polish so "it would keep forever," and china that was reserved for special occasions. Mother was so proud of the family continuity that her table represented. The vegetables were in separate china dishes, and hot rolls were in a basket with a lace roll napkin with individual compartments for each roll. I told her that the table looked beautiful.

"You know I've often wondered," said Mother as she served us sliced beef with carrots and potatoes, "why we didn't move years ago when we felt the urge to branch out. I don't know what we were afraid of. But we did seem to be afraid of so many things. I guess it was the depression. We'll never forget that. I guess the fear of it happening again made us live with a kind of lid on ourselves."

Dad plowed into his food as he usually did when Mother dominated the conversation. Even over dinner, they often seemed to me like two theatrical stars competing for the spotlight. No wonder Warren and I were actors. We had been subtly trained by two experts more dedicated to garnering attention than even the Barrymores or Redgraves. It was inevitable that I would act because I had learned early to act, not as a means of expression but as a means of communicating and getting what I wanted.

Mother served the vegetables topped with melted butter.

"Maybe I'll have another life to live after this," she said, "where I can do things right—where I won't be so afraid. I just wish that I hadn't cared so much about doing what was expected of me all my life."

I drank some ice water. She had always served sparkling ice water at a meal.

"I guess I've never been able to face realities," she continued. "I always seemed to be more interested in having fun and playing tennis when I was young. Why didn't somebody guide me in the right direction? Why did the life around me go right over my head? I remember little Howard Ulmer. We teased him because all he cared about were birds—he knew everything about them, what they ate, how they mated . . . all their habits. But he turned out to be the one who cared about something besides himself. He was *interested* in something. I know I could have been interested in something if someone had helped me. Have a hot roll, Shirl . . . I made them especially."

Daddy had nearly finished his food. "Scotch," he said, calling Mother by her nickname because she was mostly Scottish and tight with a dollar. "Now, you know Howard Ulmer wasn't just *thought* of as a fairy. He *was* a fairy. So what are you talking about?"

"I'm saying so what if he was? I don't see anything so wrong with that anyway."

We finished dinner with hot pumpkin pie Mother had baked herself. Pumpkin pie was a symbol of celebration for her. It was ceremonial and also very delicious.

"Well, Dad," I said, stalling a little and then deciding to bring it up anyway, "who did you vote for?"

He got up from the table, lit his pipe again, settled himself in his rocking chair, and looked at me.

"Oh no," I said, "you didn't."

"No, I didn't." He puffed on his pipe with a little smile. "Out of loyalty to you and Warren for working so hard I voted for McGovern. But I did it with an overwhelming sense of security that I didn't have to worry because he wasn't going to win anyway."

Mother walked across the room and turned on the television set. As the picture cleared and the sound came up, I found myself looking into my own face. *The Apartment* was on.

"What's it feel like to watch yourself like that?" she asked. "Do you know now what you could have done then to make it better? Do you look different to yourself?"

I wasn't thinking about *The Apartment*. I couldn't. I

was thinking about everything that had happened since then.

"Mother, I don't know," I said. "I was thinking about how many people in movies weren't afraid to be political this year. I was thinking how it was when a trade paper columnist used to call me a dingbat for speaking out in public."

"Why don't you go back to doing what you do best," Dad said, "and stop all this preachin' around?"

"I will," I said. "I'd love to."

I tried to explain how the state of the country had confused the writers and producers, how they didn't know any longer what was funny and what was entertaining, and certainly didn't know what to write for a woman. I thought nothing good would be made in the movies until the country was straightened out. Dad thought I was too idealistic, and Mother thought I was becoming more cynical, probably from hanging around with newspapermen. We talked like that for a while, and then we switched channels and watched the inaugural balls.

"Hail to the Chief" sounded. The camera went to the ballroom floor, where several thousand Republicans stood around, unable to move, drinking champagne out of plastic glasses decorated with the presidential seal. Women in ballgowns were crushed up against men who looked like stuffed penguins. Then quite suddenly, Nixon walked onto the ballroom stage, followed by Pat, his daughters, and Mamie Eisenhower.

"It's really too bad you didn't go, Shirl. It really would have been something to be part of."

Nixon stood by the microphone and surveyed the room, obviously in an effusive mood. This was the first time the country had seen him in public since the Christmas saturation bombing of Hanoi. His face seemed to reach for an appropriate expression as his eyes shifted under his eyebrows. Pat stood elegantly beside him, reminding herself intermittently to hold her head high.

"Well, now," said the president of the United States, "this is our first in how many balls tonight?" He began to count out loud on his fingers. "One, two, three. How many Pat—Mrs. Nixon, I mean?"

The audience waited.

"Funny," he continued, "I can't count past four!" He waited for a laugh which was strained. "Four, you know—the number *four*, that's important to me."

I looked over at Dad. He blinked and took a drag on his pipe.

"Now, I understand there has been some question as to whether or not I'll dance," Nixon continued. "Well, I like doing what I'm good at and that's not it." Another strained laugh. "I don't understand much of the music that's played today—that the youth like—mind you it's all right with me but I'm a little old-fashioned, I suppose you'd say, so if we could have something slow I'll try to do what I'm not good at."

He disappeared into a mass of bobbing heads, and I asked Dad why he thought Nixon would be a good president.

"That's easy. Because he knows so much more than McGovern about what's going on. In other words he's experienced. Since any man who wants to be president will do anything to get there, we might as well have the man who will do *anything* best."

"In other words the *best* liar, the *most* shrewdly corrupt, and so on."

"That's right."

"And you call me cynical?"

"Let me tell you a little story to illustrate my point," he said, taking the stage with one of his down-home homilies.

"There was a little girl bird who was sitting on a tree branch. She was enjoying the day and the sunshine when along flew a little boy bird and sat down beside her. How are you today? said the boy bird. Oh, just fine, just fine. Are you here alone? said the boy bird. Yes. Would you like to take a fly with me over to that big tree over there? he asked. Oh, I couldn't do that, because I'm married. Oh, well now, that *is* a difficult problem, isn't it? Yes. Do you ever cheat then? No, I don't. Then she leveled a look at him and said, But I'll hold still while you do."

I looked at Dad. "You mean Nixon is letting someone else screw him while he holds still?"

"No—I mean Nixon can cheat on us but he's smart enough to say somebody else did it."

The trumpets blared "Hail to the Chief."

The president filed in again, his mood even more ebullient.

"Hey, there," he began and immediately held up his five fingers. "How many balls have we been to? Let's see one, two, three—funny I can't count past four."

He did the exact same four-year routine again, as though the television cameras were not recording him for the nation.

The TV reporters looked slightly baffled. "We've never seen the president in such an open mood," said one of them.

"Who do we have here from California?" asked Nixon. Cheers and hands went up from his home state.

"Yeahh good—good to see ya! Nice showing out there and from New York. I just want to tell ya—(the more he spoke the more I realized his delivery was like Bob Hope's) . . . I want to thank the people of New York for all their help during a very difficult and trying time for me in the past. You were understanding and helpful and I want you to know I won't forget it. And we did well in New York, which I want to thank you for." He went on to acknowledge representatives from states along the East coast finishing with, "And who's here from Massachusetts?"

Some hands went up. "You know," he said, "we may have lost Massachusetts but I checked the figures and my percentage there this time was an improvement over 1968. I know that you'll improve next time too." He began to talk about his inability to dance well again but he would try.

Dad stared at the TV set. It didn't seem to bother him that the president of the United States, the leader of the Free World and all that, was still fighting the campaign.

Nixon remounted the stage even though "Hail to the Chief" had played his exit music.

"I want you to know, ladies and gentlemen, that I have just danced with ten young lovely ladies and none of them were over seventeen. Now if that is an example of the future of the next four years. I . . . ahh . . . well . . ." He didn't finish the sentence. Les Brown, the orchestra conductor, leaned over to him and said something. He had a microphone hanging on a wire around his neck.

"What is that, Les?" said the president. "Your *umbilical cord?* You know you're too old for that."

Pat Nixon looked stunned. The reporter covering the event was caught speechless.

Dad coughed.

"Welcome to your president, Dad," I said.

"I'm going to bed," said Mother. "He makes me sick. Ira, how could you really mean it when you say he'll make a good president? He's nothing but a fascist and you know it."

"Dad smirked at Mother's outburst.

"And you're not liberal either," she said to Dad. "You like to say you are but you're *not*! I voted the liberal ticket straight down the line but you only voted for McGovern. And for all the wrong reasons! Good night!"

She got up, stalked out of the room, and yelled back! "And Agnew makes me sicker!"

"That's why I like living with your mother," Dad said. "Wouldn't trade her in for anything. Just because she does little things like that. Why she can be a real spitfire sometimes."

We sat there for a long while, Dad and I, while Nixon moved on to more balls, and nobody asked him now how he felt about the hospitals he had bombed in Hanoi and nobody asked him about the Watergate. Nixon seemed nervous and on the edge of cracking, as if the tension within had nowhere else to go, and I felt as if I were watching a car crash. Dad started to talk about the people in the new neighborhood, and how, he said, they felt about me.

"Other people might be popular," he said. "But you're loved, and they don't think you should have

shown your tits in that nekkid scene in *Desperate Characters.*"

I wanted to laugh, but instead we talked, about
pornography and movies and image. I was, after all,
his daughter and I should realize his position. I said I
did. When the inaugural balls were finally over, Dad
and I were still talking.

"You've changed a lot, with this work you've been
doing in politics," he said.

"Yeah, I guess so. So have you."

"You're easier to talk to."

"So are you."

"I guess there's a lot to be said for idealism being
practical—maybe. Maybe it's not so idealistic to want
what you want."

"What do you want, Dad?"

He sighed and thought a moment. "When I die, I'd
like to die knowing that I did something to make the
world a better place. You know, maybe I helped someone or something . . .'"

I kissed him good night and went to bed happy.
Somehow, in some important way, we had finally made
real contact. I had believed for a long time that we
held almost diametrically opposing points of view, and
that perhaps my values had evolved as a protest and
rebuttal against his. Essentially, and in practice, I guess
that was true but, for a little while on that night, we
had agreed with each other.

The next morning it rained. Rumpled but happy, Dad
strolled into the sun room. "I'm trying to decide if I'm
alive or not," he said. "And I guess the answer is that's

all there is." He sat down in his rocking chair and looked out the window. "Have you seen our white pigeons?"

"Where?"

"Oh, they come around all the time. They never leave each other. One won't let the other out of its sight. They need each other. They're beautiful. You watch and you'll see them."

An hour later the white pigeons came. They darted and swooped and played in and out of the falling rain, gurgling and nuzzling each other, and never let each other out of sight.

"You see," said Mother. "They will always be together." We watched silently.

With my bags packed, they walked me to the car. The street was shiny with rain.

"Will you come back again when we're seventy-one?" said Mother.

"I sure will," I said, "but remember when I do, I'll be almost forty."

There was a long pause.

"You've had quite a life haven't you?" said Dad. "And quite a year."

"Yep, but not like what's coming up next month."

"What's that?"

"I'm going to China."

His jaw dropped. "You're going to see the Commies in China?"

"Yep."

"Jesus Christ, and I thought McGovern was bad."

"Yep."

"Why? Why are you going?" He seemed threatened and excited at the same time.

"Because it's there."

"Oh. The same reason you and the other guy climbed those Hymalayas, eh?"

"Something like that."

There was nothing more to say. Mother said she was thrilled for me and told me to be careful.

They were standing together in the doorway as I drove away, waving good-by. I thought about the pigeons.

Fifteen

I HAD DREAMED of China since childhood. It was a strange vast space on the maps, in geography books, or a place that might be within reach if you could only dig deep enough in the backyard. It was a mysterious place, a symbol of the unreachable and the remote, a place to which only a privileged few had traveled. Then when I was a teenager, the papers were suddenly full of news about China. My parents would talk about how we had "lost" China to the Communists, and I would ask them when it had been ours to lose, and they would tell me it was too complicated to explain.

Later, as I grew up and got on with my life in show business, I read horror stories in *Time* magazine about people who had been reduced to ants in a faceless place called Red China. I was told that the real China was a place called Formosa, which looked to me like an off-shore island when I studied a map. People were saying that the Red Chinese were certain to come ashore some night on the Pacific coast and conquer all the American supermarkets and invade private houses, or something like that.

In 1953, I read a book called *The Sands of Karakorum* by James Ramsey Ullman, about a Western couple who disappeared into the heart of China while searching for a reason and purpose in life. A friend went after them, plunging into the vast emptiness of those spaces of sand and moaning wind. The book made me feel somehow

that in China I could get closer to myself. Later, I would
stand at the Kowloon Bridge staring across at the green
hills trying to imagine what China was like.

Once, high in the Himalayas, as I watched the sun
rise, I felt a sudden urge to leap right over Mount Kan-
chenjunga, and into China on the other side. Several
times I had thought of getting a forged passport in
Hong Kong, and once actually had it arranged, but then
didn't go through with it because I was afraid I'd lose
my real passport. Instead, I went to China via books,
traveling with Edgar Snow, and Pearl Buck, Felix Green
and Ross Terrill, and most of all with my friend Han
Suyin.

More and more, I wanted the real thing. I wanted
to see China the way I had seen Japan and Africa and
India and all the countries of Europe. I wanted to know
about the revolution, see for myself what had happened
over the last twenty years in a country of 800,000,000
people. Through newspapers I had followed the course
of the Cultural Revolution. I had listened to Japanese
newsmen who told me that something really new was
happening in China. The something new, they claimed,
was that China was becoming the first country in modern times to truly revolutionize human beings. I wanted
to see that. And then, in 1972, China opened up.

When the members of the Permanent Mission to the
United Nations of the People's Republic of China ar-
rived in New York in October 1971, Princess Ashraf
Pahlavi of Iran invited me to a luncheon in their honor.
The politics of the Shah of Iran were not the politics of
Mao Tse-tung, to say the least, but at the luncheon we
didn't talk much about politics. Over a period of three

hours, we talked about human beings, their capacity for change and growth, their personal development, and what China was doing about such matters. And before the luncheon was over, I had been invited to visit China.

The man who did the inviting was Chiao Kuan Hua, the foreign minister. "It's very important for the American people to understand China," he said, speaking through an interpreter (even though he spoke perfect English). "We need much improvement. It is impossible for others to observe what we are trying to do in a short period of time, because it has taken us forty years of revolution to come to where we are now, trying to understand ourselves along the way. We hope your people will be as patient as we have been with ourselves."

He inhaled the smoke of a Chinese cigarette called a Panda, daintily holding the cigarette as so many Asians do. His legs were crossed, and he balanced a demitasse gingerly on one knee. "Actors and actresses and writers," he said, "are capable of influencing masses of people *and* public opinion, because they represent what the people want. And they are loved besides. I think it would be a good idea for you to come to China."

The invitation was extended, and eventually was expanded. I was to lead the first American women's delegation to China. I could come with a party of twelve, including a crew who would film what we saw. The only specification was that the women should be "regular." That was a difficult word to interpret, but I worked with mounting excitement to assemble a group of "regular" women. The Chinese did not want celebrities, with the exception of myself; they did not ask for a collection of

Marxists, or a group of doctors, or a troupe of radicals. They wanted "regular" women. And over the following months, I invited the following women:

Unita Blackwell, a 200-pound, coal black woman of mammoth heart, who came from Issaquena County, Mississippi. I had met her on a voter-registration drive during the 1960s. She lived then in a home without running water, with a tin roof, an outside toilet, a battered Dodge in the driveway, and a TV set in the living room. The Ku Klux Kan's local chapter burned crosses on her lawn because I had stayed in her house, but Unita seemed to rise above such occurrences. After I had invited her to come to China, and she recovered from the shock, Unita told me that her social life had drastically changed; she was now being invited to the white folks' homes, because nobody could believe that Unita Blackwell actually was going to China.

Patricia Branson, a thirty-three-year-old clerk in the Texaco Oil Company in Port Arthur, Texas, was a strong union member and a conservative Democrat who believed, when I first met her, that George Wallace would be the savior of America. Pat was a flirt, always dressed to kill, with a beehive of jet black teased hair and layers of carefully applied make-up. She had a great sense of humor, which was often directed at herself. Her neat house, in a lower-middle-class section of Port Arthur, contained a stereo set, candles carved in the shape of Buddhas, and shelves bulging with knickknacks. She hated George McGovern, thought the Democratic convention was a disgrace (because of "abortion and faggots and Mexicans), and was convinced that Henry Kissinger and Richard Nixon were Communists. I liked her immediately. When I asked her to make the trip to China, she wanted to know if the trip was OK with the government. At that time, of course, the government was run by Richard Nixon and Henry Kissinger, the Communists.

Rosa Marin, a wise, mature fifty-two-year-old writer and sociologist from the University of Puerto Rico in San Juan, was recommended by friends as a superb researcher. Rosa was soft-spoken and introverted. She had worked hard for the people of Puerto Rico and wanted to learn from the Chinese. "I am interested in anything that is human," she said.

Ninibah Crawford, a tawny-skinned Navaho Indian beauty with eyes like moist black olives, worked for the Bureau of Indian Affairs on a reservation in Arizona. She was about thirty-three and lived in a trailer with two children from a dissolved marriage. She worshipped nature, and once, while driving me through deep snow to see her parents in their traditional hogan, she talked with some bitterness about the sordid history of the white man's treatment of the American Indian. She rejoiced at the prospect of the China trip, saying that "nature will be even more beautiful there than what we have here."

Karine Boutilier, a twelve-year-old schoolgirl from Racine, Wisconsin, was working as a grape boycott organizer for the United Farm Workers Union when I met her during the McGovern campaign. She was poised and diplomatic on the telephone, and seemed like a good choice for the journey. In the months between invitation and departure, she set about getting her first passport, had me explain the trip to her parents, and arranged with the principal of her school to take off the necessary time from school.

Phyllis Kronhausen, a psychologist, cultural anthropologist, and an old, dear friend. Phyllis was forty years old and had grown up on a Minnesota farm. She was interested in the broad subject of human freedom and wanted to see what the Chinese people were doing on an interpersonal level. She was particularly interested in sexuality in China. She and her husband, Dr. Eberhard Kronhausen, had written a number of books on erotic art, sexual fantasies, pornograhy and the law, and marriage. Phyllis was essentially a soft, caring person, with a brilliant mind, but she could be incisive and tough when asking questions. I thought she would also be useful in the event of culture shock among other members of the delegation, many of whom had never left their home towns.

Margaret Whitman. She was the last to be chosen, but certainly not the least. Toward the end of the selection process, I decided I needed a conservative Republican housewife person, someone who was affluent, who loved athletics, the flag, capitalism, and the POWs. I didn't know anybody like that, but I started asking around. Margaret, arriving from Long Island, swept into my New York apartment as if she were about to ride to the hounds. "You're taking me with you," she said firmly. "My name is Whitman, and I'm just what you're looking for. I'm conservative, tweedy, self-sufficient, and way over thirty." I liked her—after all, she *insisted* on it.

The rest of the delegation was composed of filmmakers. Since I was bringing a women's delegation, I wanted a crew of women. I had seen Claudia Weill's fine documentary, *Joyce at 34,* and knew that she had served as cinematographer on a film called *Year of the Woman,* made by Sandra Hochman at the Democratic National Convention. Claudia was young, strong, and

healthy. She was accustomed to carrying and running
with a thirty-five-pound camera, and could cope with the
long shooting days we would have in China; I wanted the
crew to photograph China by day, and the women's
reactions to China at night. Claudia thought of herself
as a feminist, had read *Fanshen*, William Hinton's clas-
sic study of the effect of the revolution on a Chinese
village, and was bursting with enthusiasm to make the
journey.

Over a period of a few weeks, Claudia and I inter-
viewed scores of young women who wanted to go to
China as part of our four-woman crew. Claudia asked
all the technical questions; I asked the personal questions.

In the end, we picked Nancy Shreiber, twenty-four,
one of the best electrical technicians in New York, who
also held a B.A. in psychology; Cabell Glickler, thirty,
the only woman in the sound union in New York, who
was employed by NBC and deeply interested in medita-
tion, the East, and yoga; and Joan Weidman, a tall, thin
woman of twenty-two, who was the youngest member of
the crew, and operated an Eclair camera. Claudia would
operate the first camera, Joan the second camera, while
Nancy handled the lighting and the electrical problems,
and Cabell the sound.

The crew members were all feminists, but they were
also individuals with their own special personalities and
concerns. Claudia was sensitive and aware to the point
of self-consciousness, worrying a little too much about
looking "too Jewish." Nancy worked in blue jeans, listened intently, and then spoke in short machine-gun-
like bursts. Cabell was pleasant, freshly scrubbed, and

giggled like a musical comedy star. She was sufficiently
anxious about her job at NBC to pass on their request
to me to explain the mission, its purpose, whether it
was approved by the United States government, and
what we would do in China. We told them nothing.
Joan Weidman was a militant feminist who seemed extraordinarily strong, as if she had made her thin body
into a tool through an act of will.

We got to know each other slowly, and then, on
April 16, 1973, we left New York.

When we arrived at Los Angeles International Airport
we were greeted by a barrage of flashbulbs and cameras
and a flood of questions from reporters. "I keep pinching
myself," said Karen, "to make sure it's real." Rosa said,
"To learn is to be human. I want to do both." Pat
Branson winked at the reporters: "Hi, yawl. I think the
way you Democrats treated George Wallace was just
pitiful. But I want to go to China to see the oil interests.
I work at the Texaco plant down home in Texas and I
hope they don't dock my salary while I'm gone."

Did I really hear Pat say those things? Was she really
talking about seeing the "oil interests" in China? She
was.

"I've been accused of bein' a Communist for so long,"
Unita said. "So I want to go to China to see what one
a them Communists looks like."

Claudia and the crew lugged the rigging lights, the
tie-in cables, the metal camera boxes, the light plugs, and
five cameras onto the TWA jet that would take us across
the Pacific. They were dressed in overalls that made
them look like people from the water and power com-

pany. Pat Branson lugged two suitcases, one full of keys
to the city of Port Arthur, some small Texas flags, Texaco
piggy banks, and the other full of make-up.

We settled into the plane, with Joan, Nancy, and
Cabell jammed against the bulkhead with their 2000
pounds of equipment. Claudia sat with her camera in
her lap, biting her nails, lost in concentration or reverie.
Rosa read a novel. Karen got airsick and then fell asleep.
Pat wrote postcards to her husband and flirted with two
sailors. Unita sat beside Pat, kidding her, and Margaret
told the sailors to forget about those Southern belles—
regardless of race, color, and creed—and try *her*, because
she was more experienced than all of them.

America disappeared behind us as we paradoxically
flew west to get to the Far East. Honolulu provided an
hour of paradise. Guam was a military disaster. And the
Pacific was very wide. We had begun a journey that
would cover thousands of miles, and we would be together in places stranger to us than any we could have
dreamed of. I hoped that the trip would be the best of
all journeys: a journey into ourselves.

It was to be a journey to the interior, all right, but not
the one I had hoped for.

Sixteen

In Hong Kong, the women seemed bowled over by the Far East. For a full day, they plunged into the markets, breathed the smells of the Orient, and embraced the exotic town with the same kind of excitement and fervor I had experienced fifteen years earlier. They didn't seem to notice the pollution and the noise; they couldn't recognize the deterioration in quality. They hadn't been in Hong Kong in the old days; they didn't know what it had once been. And I wondered, late in the afternoon, whether it was Hong Kong that had changed, or whether it was me, or perhaps both. Maybe I had wandered the world in a kind of freewheeling cocoon when I was younger, concerned more about myself and my adventures than I was in what I was seeing. Maybe it had always been noisy, overpopulated, and polluted.

The women bought clothes, luxuriated in the sensuality of the silks and brocades, and lovingly touched the hand-made objects. I could see myself in them, that part of me that was still a wide-eyed American, that part of me that had been educated to give value to material possessions. Karen bought all her gifts at the first stop in the Orient. Pat loved the carved Buddhas. She talked about how she missed her daughter, but didn't want to spend the rest of the day taking care of Karen. Unita was homesick too, and was keeping her watch on Mississippi time. However, she loved every homesick minute.

"If getting shot at, because I wanted to vote, is what got me here," she said, "then I'd be perfectly willing to do it all over again."

Claudia and the crew started photographing the others, and sure enough, as soon as the red light went on, they began to overact. It would take time to relax.

We all had lunch on a harbor yacht called the *Wan Fu*, where we were served from silver hot plates and drank from crystal glasses, while moving past junks crowded with burnt-out, sun-bleached laundry and the hills behind the city climbing like peopled stairways in the distance. This was not, to me, the first step into China; no, Hong Kong was the last outpost of the West, and the ruined values of the West were all around us: the jangling aggressiveness of the marketplace, the faces scarred by greed and avarice. The harsh voices of people pitted against one another for economic survival.

"It's a dream," Unita said, interrupting my reverie. "Me, from the plantations of Mississippi—am I *really* sailing the China Seas?"

We all laughed. I felt strange. When we came back to the dock, we peeled off alone; some to find a private spot on the dock where we could soak up the sun, others to explore the intricate alleys of the waterfront. The women with me had already left their own familiar world. Tomorrow I would be leaving a familiar world too. I looked over and saw Unita pull a scarf from her bag and cover her hair. Her wig had blown off. I laughed and lay back with my eyes closed. In the morning I felt that somehow I would be going home, back where I had never been.

The railway station at Kowloon was a wild and frantic crush of travelers, reporters, and baggage. Most of it seemed to be *our* baggage: mounds of it, boxes of it, 2000 pounds of equipment, and fifteen suitcases. The representatives of the China Travel Service were politely restrained, but obviously overwhelmed by our impediment. The aggressive Hong Kong journalists, most of them Chinese, chased after us as we shouted apologies and waved at them from the train. I took a seat by a window, and soon many Chinese were tapping on the glass, trying to send messages to relatives on the Mainland. Their eyes were full of the sorrow and regret that you always see in people who are exiles.

Slowly, the train began to move. We had started. We were going into China through Shumchun, a few miles on the other side of Kowloon, where we would go through passport and customs controls. An hour and a half later we arrived at the border. On the British side, we looked across the railway bridge. Dense crowds of foreigners were making their way across the bridge, many of them visitors returning from the Canton Trade Fair, which was then in progress. Suddenly we found ourselves in a swirl of Westerners and Chinese who were pushing and lifting and maneuvering our cases, packages, cameras, presents, hats, and passports. Chinese workers strung suitcase after suitcase along resilient bamboo poles, and shuffled with them to the British customs shed. It was clear to me that we would never be able to keep track of the luggage. That would require an act of faith.

The British customs people were friendly and efficient. And then, quite suddenly, we were finished. Twenty steps away was the border bridge. Claudia and Joan ran ahead to film us as we crossed. This was it: the step forward into the blank spaces on all those schoolroom maps, the place where the New Man was being built, the

place where those travelers had lost themselves in the
Sands of Karakorum, the country of "Man's Fate" and
the Dowager Queen, the Ming Tombs and the Great
Wall. At a few minutes after eleven thirty A.M. on April
20 I stepped into the mystery that had haunted me for
most of my adult life.

The world changed immediately. In the Chinese
customs area, at the far side of the bridge, Red Army
men wearing red stars on their hats, and rumpled green
uniforms inspected our passports. Behind them, a wall
poster in English said "People of the World, Unite."

The frantic commercial jangle of Hong Kong was
gone. Instead there was a quiet, almost serene quality to
the atmosphere. People spoke in muted voices, and
huge, big-leaved trees rustled over the railroad tracks.
There was a sense of peace, and of safety, and it was
immediately infectious; I found myself speaking in a
quieter tone, and so did the other women.

We sat in a bright sunlit room with right-angled furniture and white covers on the chairs. In a corner, a
thermos and tea cups sat on a dresser, and there were
copies of *China Reconstructs* and *China Pictorial*, official English-language magazines of the Chinese government. We met our two guides and interpreters. Yeh
Sing Ru had short, cropped hair, glasses, and a business-
like demeanor she frequently broke with a mischievous
smile. Chang Chingerh was older, perhaps in her mid-
forties, with huge brown eyes and gray-streaked dark
hair tied in a bun. All of us shook hands and introduced
ourselves, and then we filled in all the customs forms,
declaring money, jewelry, tape recorders, film, and even
magazines. I asked Chang how I should declare the
movie equipment.

"No problem, I don't think," she said. "How much do you have?"

"Two thousand pounds of various things."

Her face went blank. For a moment I panicked; maybe they hadn't expected all this equipment, maybe my letters explaining what we were bringing had never arrived, or had been bogged down in bureaucratic red tape. I remembered one unhappy trip I had made to the Soviet Union a decade before, when any possible feelings of friendship had been stifled because of a hostile customs search.

"Come then," Chang said with a shrug. The firmness in her voice made me relax. I followed her into the customs building, to be greeted by a huge idealized portrait of Mao Tse-tung as a young man, dressed in long student robes which flapped in a sea breeze that I could almost feel. He wore one of those wise, almost beatific expressions that you see in bad paintings of Jesus Christ. I turned a corner, following the efficient Chang, and was greeted with another portrait of Mao. This was in more modern times, and Mao was wearing a Western white shirt and trousers, surveying his liberated land, while smoking a cigarette. For some reason, the portrait looked like one of those Camel ads that used to run on the back of the *Saturday Evening Post*. Sitting directly beneath the painting, holding his cigarette in exactly the same way Mao was holding his, was a Chinese businessman from Hong Kong. Life was imitating art, just as it so often did in the West.

On the other side of the room was still another portrait of the Chairman, this one huge and in close-up. His mole was as large as my hand. A poster instructed all of us, in screaming white block letters, to "Work Hard for the Continuing Revolution to Accomplish Even Greater

Victories." In addition to the portraits of Mao, there were pictures of Karl Marx, Friedrich Engels, and Joseph Stalin.

While Chang poured over the customs forms for us, I watched the other travelers. Impeccably dressed black men from Mali were speaking quietly in French. An American woman in her sixties told me her interest in China dated back to Kansas City, where a nice Chinese man had done her husband's shirts! Chinese peasant travelers, hunkering down on their haunches, smoked in silence.

There were no hawkers selling goods, no frenzied bargaining. Nobody was buying and nobody was selling. And because of that, I could hear birds singing in the trees. Chang came out of an office, holding some papers.

"Yes," she said. "I see what you mean."

She had rounded up several customs agents, who were now looking at the strange boxes while Claudia, Joan, Cabell, and Nancy explained their contents. The crew seemed slightly dazed.

"I can't remember," Claudia said, "which is in which case. We changed so many things around last night in Hong Kong."

I asked her if all the equipment was there.

"I don't know," she said.

"Have you declared each of these pieces?" one of the female customs officers asked.

"Yes."

"OK," she said to Chang. "You may proceed."

Yeh smiled and said, "Sure—no sweat."

Obviously we were not the first Americans she had dealt with.

The train to Canton took us through a landscape of

smooth, eye-caressing serenity. For the first time I began
to realize that China was a place of absences; a Westerner
would eventually define it by noting what was *not* there.
We passed farmland, and farmers who dotted the land
in all directions. There were no billboards screaming out
their false promises, no slums, no sense of that rundown
deprivation one usually finds alongside railroad tracks.
Serene, I said to myself. That is the word. Serene.

The train was a thing of beauty. Each seat was covered
with a white lace cover, there were folding tables of dark
wood, an air conditioner gently whirred, and an aria
from the Peking Revolutionary Opera was being played
on the train loud-speaker. I noticed a small button beside my table, turned it, and the sound diminished.
Apparently, it required only one dissident to soften the
sound of revolutionary music.

The women heaved their hand luggage up onto the
overhead racks (the heavy baggage was handled else-
where) and sat back to watch the rice paddies and the
shade trees as we moved deeper into China. I remembered seeing countryside like this in India, but there was
a crucial difference; in China, nobody seemed to be
resting.

We planned the hotel living arrangements during the
trip to Canton. I had worked out a rotating arrangement
whereby each person would have a different roommate
in each city. I hoped that the women thus would get to
know each other more intimately, and the flow of reactions among them would be periodically refreshed. The
members of the film crew would not rotate with the
others, because they said they needed close nightly contact in which to discuss the numerous technical details
that go with making a full-legnth film that does not have

a script. I decided to room for the entire trip with Phyllis
Kronhausen, who was an old friend. I wanted time to
make decisions for the delegation as a whole, since I had
been its leader from the beginning. I also felt I needed
privacy. And this need for privacy—the most Western
requirement of the individual—was later to cause problems.

The results were that we were splitting into two delegations, although I did not realize it then. The first
delegation included Unita, Pat, Ninibah, Rosa, Karen,
and Margaret. The four-woman crew and Phyllis and I
formed another. The first delegation was being studied
by the second delegation, and as we traveled together,
we started to grow apart.

But on that first day, everything was the wonder of a
new world opening up to us. It would be a grand adventure, a trip motivated by hope. I could hear Margaret
and Unita talking together behind me.

"When I saw those Orientals with uniforms back at
the border," said Margaret, "it did something to my
stomach. Whether Japanese or Chinese, I saw so much
of what Orientals did in New Guinea and Leyte when
I was out there during the war. I guess it will take me a
while to get over it."

"Yeah, honey," said Unita, "but just look at them out
there working. They don't even have no plows. They
doing it all with elbow grease." She rose up on one arm
and gazed out. "Boy, the first part of my life weren't too
good—but the Bible must have said someplace in it that
I was going to China."

Seventeen

I T W A S R A I N I N G when we arrived in Canton. Not a simple spring shower, but a great, heavy dense tropical rain. It came down in opaque sheets, blinding the view, hiding the buildings, bending the trunks of the lush green trees. It was a monsoon rain, the kind of rain I had seen in the Philippines, and it fed the trees and pounded on the tin roofs of the buildings at the railroad station.

There were reporters here too, from a Canton TV station. Claudia and the crew jumped out to take advantage of their lights on this day so dark with tropical rain. The Chinese TV men crowded in, examining our equipment, surprised at its weight, and even more surprised that a group of women was handling the heavier American equipment with such apparent ease. "Well, if you can carry this stuff," one man said in English, "and *run* at the same time, I guess we can too."

The station was like a set from an old Warner Brothers movie about intrigue on the China coast. The waiting room was full of rattan tables and chairs, fans whirred on the low-slung ceiling, and gray was the pervasive color except for the ubiquitous portraits of Mao Tsetung. I was starting to get used to his face now, and as we walked to our bus, I raised my fist at him in a salute, and winked.

Our equipment was being loaded onto a bus backed up to the station platform, and a small, neat, buck-toothed man named Mister Woo came toward us. He was from the China Travel Agency and he and his associates walked right past me to Pat Branson. The leader of this delegation, after all, was an actress and with all that piled hair and layered make-up, Pat apparently looked like the only actress in the group. Chang and Yeh came over and intercepted Mister Woo quickly. We shook hands.

The bus moved out, and took us into Canton, a city of 2,000,000, all of whom seemed to be riding bicycles. The rain began to slacken. It was a city of two- and three-story buildings, with some larger buildings that I later discovered were hotels. The traffic ebbed and flowed around us, and I looked down the side streets, which were clean and crowded, and saw lush tropical vegetation everywhere. Trees arched over the sidewalks, and there were British colonial-style verandahs on most of the buildings to protect the citizens from the frequent heavy rains. I could smell Chinese vegetables cooking in soy sauce, and was struck by the vast sameness of clothing among the Cantonese: the men wore gray or blue "Mao suits," the women trousers of the same colors. A few people were barefoot, but most wore sandals. The rain stopped as we pulled up to the hotel.

Through all of this, Pat flirted wildly with Mister Woo, winking at him, laughing at his jokes, and giggling at his explanations. When he dropped us at the hotel, he eased away from us, pointed out the Pearl River, which flowed in front of the modern building, and escaped. Pat smiled. She seemed to sense that, one way or another, she had made contact with something beneath Mister Woo's revolutionary spirit.

Our footsteps echoed through the large hollow lobby.

To the right there was a money exchange, and another small counter where postcards and stamps were sold. Visitors to the trade fair moved around us, complaining about prices ("The prices are a hundred per cent higher this year; the Chinese are no better off than we are") or buying souvenirs. I started to talk to some of these people, when Nancy suddenly took my arm.

"Jesus Christ," she said. "We don't have the right lighting equipment. The plugs I brought don't fit. The electricians in New York and Hong Kong were wrong about what sockets China uses."

No plugs, no lights. No lights, no movie. We checked our gear and then went outside to find a department store that might have the right plugs. We were on our own, since Chang and Yeh had gone to the manager's office.

On the street, we were an instant curiosity. We were immediately surrounded by a crowd, a quiet crowd that studied our shoes, our hair, our clothes, our unfamiliar round eyes. We stared back, searching faces, looking for contact; we were as curious about the people of China as they were about us. Bike riders stopped and joined the throng; others on foot stopped abruptly and came to stare at the group of Western women.

The rain continued, light and soft now. I walked over to one young woman and put out my hand. She backed up, shyly, almost nervously, not looking at the others, just as the others did not look at her. And then, concentrating very hard on my face, she reached out and touched my hand.

That was the first contact, as tentative and curious as the contact being made on the world stage between our two giant countries. I did not know the woman's name;

she did not know mine. But we had touched each other.

The crowd was really large now, halting traffic. I wrote on a sheet of paper: "Hello, I am glad to meet you," on the unlikely chance that someone might be able to read English. There were giggles, probably over the strangeness of the Western scribble, and everyone waited for me to write something else. I did. Again, there was laughter. Then we seemed to be moving together. We moved a few steps, and the crowd moved with us, as if not wanting to miss a gesture or a smile. It did not seem possible that those in the back could actually see us, but they did not push forward for a better view. They seemed to accept the fact that whoever was in front was in front. The experience was eerie but somehow comforting. In other countries I'd visited, even among primitive African tribes who had never seen a white person before, there was a strong individual drive and people would strain or push to see a newcomer for themselves— to get in front. Not in China.

We began to edge our way to the People's Department Store, three blocks away. The crowd opened and let us pass. And as we walked along, talking about the experience, they followed us.

The shoppers in the dimly lit department store seemed startled when we entered. Unita's wig was drying somewhere, and her head was plaited with Afro pigtails; she was, well, *impressive*, as she moved from counter to counter in this Chinese department store, fondling the silks. Huge wooden earrings dangled from her ears. Pat was wearing a crimson red Chinese brocade slack suit she had bought in Hong Kong, and which looked like the prime reason the Chinese had their revolution in the

first place. The Chinese women stared at her beehive
hairdo nervously, as if expecting it to topple over. Karen
dashed into the children's department and bought an
entire Mao outfit—jacket, slacks, cap, and button—and
changed her clothes on the spot.

At one point, the lights in the store dimmed even
more. "I guess they need a good electrician," said electrician Nancy, as we waited for our eyes to adjust to the
darkness. Then the lights came on again. Yeh had caught
up with us now, to help translate, and she explained
that such dim-outs were frequent, "to conserve electricity."

In the appliance department, we got bad news. The
plugs weren't our basic problem; China was on a different
voltage than we were in America. The man in the appliance section altered every plug we had, but it did no
good. He shook his head sadly, and the crowd around
us seemed to sense our disappointment. They looked
from him to us for our reaction.

Nancy was upset and so was I. If we could not use
public electricity, our only source of power would be our
battery belts, which ran only one half hour each and
took fourteen hours to recharge. We left the store
quickly.

This was serious. I knew, because of my election campaigning, that some events simply do not *happen* unless
they are recorded. They are like the proverbial tree in the
forest; if it falls, and nobody is there to hear it, does it
make a noise? Without electrical power, we could not
record our journey. Any hope of making China acces-
sible to all those Western women and men who could
not visit the country themselves would be lost. I rushed

into the hotel lobby, where our luggage was still piled high. Our mounds of equipment would mean nothing unless we could bring them to life with electricity.

Then, at the elevator, I was confronted by Ninibah. The expression around her mouth was petulant.

"Why don't I have a room overlooking the river?" she complained.

I told her that several of us didn't have views and besides I had a problem with plugs and we could straighten out the rooms some other time. I went up to my room to call Chang.

The room was not impressive: it was a marble-floored square box with twin cots covered with sheets and plain gray towels for spreads. It had a view of the river. I went to the bathroom to wash my face and found the floor streaked with dirt, the tub grimy. In the medicine cabinet, there was a bar of clear yellow soap, a large green comb, and a clean glass. Slowly I washed my face. When I finished I called Chang. She said she would find an electrician for us.

We were in a city now, and the noises of a city drifted up to the room. Horns honked as incessantly as in Rome. Bicycle bells competed with the shifting of gears. I worried about the plugs, the failure of the Chinese to understand that we were shooting a film, and the resentment in Ninibah's eyes. I thought about all this, and then fell asleep on the small hard cot and did not wake up until dawn.

Early the next morning, Nancy called to tell me that our problems were solved. Chang had found an electrician who could cope with the situation and who would travel with us for the entire trip. Now we could con-

centrate on China. And promptly at 7:30, we had our
first briefing by a people's revolutionary committee. The
committee, made up equally of men and women, sat
around a long table, while our delegation took notes or
operated tape recorders. In our bright magentas, yellows,
and greens, we looked like a Forty-second Street neon
extravaganza against the muted grays and blues of the
Chinese.

The committee members started to speak about production figures and the indices of success since the liberation, passing out Panda cigarettes while they talked,
and filling cups with steaming tea. We began by sipping
quietly like good Americans, but when we noticed the
Chinese slurping their tea, we slurped ours.

A Chinese briefing is a formidable experience, and in
the weeks that followed we went through many of them.
The visitor is hit with a volley of facts, figures, and statistics, all delivered without notes and in a spirit of intense
pride. Tea, or steaming hot water, is always provided,
along with cigarettes, and always there is the portrait of
Mao, beaming and genial. On this first morning, we
were drilled with statistics serving one basic function: to
inform us of the great advances China had made since
the revolution. Before the revolution, for example, Canton was a city with only a sprinkling of light industry;
now there was heavy machinery industry, much ship-
building, and a chemical industry. There were thirty-two
urban communes in the city and their productivity increased every year.

In this briefing, as in all the others, we learned how
the area was organized, either as a factory, a commune,
or a residential district, with the citizens broken down
into families, production teams, production brigades,

revolutionary committees, and street committees. In all cases, political education was combined with such concerns as cleaning the neighborhood, human hygiene, sanitation problems, and handling personal matters, such as divorce.

I took voluminous notes, and the other women listened intently. For a while. I looked over at Pat. She had told me that morning that she wasn't eating. It seemed incredible, but Pat had *never* eaten Chinese food before in her life. She did not think there was a way "to screw up a egg," as she put it, "but Shirley, they were swimmin' in oil this morning, and the bacon was half-cooked, and the boiled eggs was raw." I had thought the Chinese porridge, with meat and vegetables, was good; Pat thought it wasn't the sort of thing you had for breakfast and had ordered bacon and eggs. She wasn't alone. The other women had complained too, and most had eaten only the thick slices of bread, smeared with great globs of butter and jelly. Pat had discovered fresh cucumbers though. They were familiar and therefore all right. But now her eyes were glazed, as much from her cucumber diet as from the onslaught of statistics.

As the briefing ended and we rose from our hard-backed chairs, it was hard to find meaning in what we had just heard. We were women from America. In America, by custom we were not expected to be involved in matters like the statistics of growth, the need for heavy machinery, and the problems of feeding millions of people. In the West, women discussed specifics that related to them personally. In China everyone sat down to tea and discussed progress, statistics, and output. The Chinese were developing a new society, and there seemed time for little else. We shook hands, thanked each other, and said good-by. Pat walked alone, dreaming of scrambled eggs and grits I supposed.

There were two Red Army soldiers with bayonets guarding the entrance to the Canton Trade Fair, a semiannual event that had begun in 1957 to promote Chinese industry and agriculture. A massive poster hung high over the group of traders on the floor of the main room, proclaiming in several languages, "The danger of a new world war still exists, and the people of all countries must be prepared. But revolution is the main trend in the world today." As always, Mao's picture smiled from one wall, and Lenin, Stalin, Marx, and Engels looked down across from him.

We were given the choice of visiting the displays featuring heavy industry, light industry, farm equipment, or arts and crafts. We voted for arts and crafts. Instead, we were deftly maneuvered toward the display of farm equipment. There were brightly lit scale models of communes, complete with irrigation schemes and planting patterns, and a woman briefed us on the glories of rice, corn, and fruit crops. Our American women were fidgeting. Most of us were city people, and food was something that came from a supermarket. The Chinese seemed puzzled at our lack of interest. For the Chinese, food was a miracle. To us, it was something that came so easily we seldom questioned its source.

The women from our delegation started to drift away, looking for things of greater interest. I watched Chang and Yeh watch us drift. They said nothing. Clearly they were not surprised.

We found the arts and crafts section. The glass display cases were filled with beauty—enamel bracelets studded with gold and precious stones; carved jade; elaborate ivory earrings; ruby and jade necklaces, shimmering and gorgeous on beds of moss green velvet. Yeh and Chang smiled at us.

"Are you interested in jewelry like this?" I asked them.

"No," said Chang. "Such trinkets prevent us from working well. They get in our way when we move about."

Would she like to own some of the beautiful things in these cases, all of which were for export only?

"They are beautiful," she said, "but as I said, they would be difficult to wear and do my work well."

It was as simple as that. I did not sense any doubt, regret, or hypocrisy in Chang's voice. All around her, we were oohing and aahing over the jewelry, as if we had walked into Tiffany's. Even when Chang said, "Women from the outside world are always interested in beautiful jewelry and silks and brocades, and men want new technological inventions that can make work and money and profit go much faster," she did not seem dogmatic or sarcastic. It was as though she was summing up the differences between her world and ours.

It seemed a pretty fair summing up of two thousand years of Western civilization.

At the trade fair, I watched the Chinese deal with the Arab, French, Italian, and American merchants, most of whom seemed continuously impatient over deals that had gone wrong, took too much time, or had become too expensive. The Chinese looked on blandly as their interpreters explained the objections, and then leaned back, almost patronizingly, to smoke their cigarettes. They didn't seem particularly interested in the money, and certainly they had time working for them. If a deal wasn't settled in the first five minutes, they could always wait. In addition to time, they had the State on their side.

I asked one Chinese merchant if the buying and selling at the fair was a form of capitalism.

"No," he said, "it's mutual exchange."

Eighteen

THE NEXT AFTERNOON in Canton, we went by bus to visit the East-Is-Red Nursery School to see the way China was bringing up its children. Five of us on the delegation had had children, seven had not, but all of us, including twelve-year-old Karen, had ideas about the way children should be raised, and as American women sometimes wondered whether the American way was correct. We looked forward to the trip. We might not be very interested in the construction of a lathe factory, but the treatment of children was another matter.

At the school we were greeted by the teachers, most of whom were middle-aged. On the school grounds were hundreds of little children, two, three, and four years old, singing together and playing on swings. When they saw us they rushed forward, chanting in Chinese, "Welcome Aunties, Welcome Aunties." The children wore lipstick and rouge, they looked like dolls. Laughing and smiling as if they knew they were meant to be adorable, they clapped their hands and shouted their welcomes. It was as if we had been overrun by an army of living dolls.

Our delegation moved along into a schoolroom. There the children stood and applauded, and waited until all of us had found a place to stand before they sat down again. They began the class by associating words with pictures, without the instruction of a teacher. The teacher then stepped into the circle of children and read a story about a young boy who had fallen down and hurt himself and needed the help of a neighbor. When she had finished, she asked for suggestions about how to help the boy, and all hands went up. The teacher listened carefully as the children enthusiastically contributed ideas. They were learning several things: how to communicate, how to help one another, and how to solve a problem. I remembered all the classroom hours I had spent as a child, memorizing theoretical answers to theoretical questions, where the purpose of giving the right answer was to pass on to the next grade. I tried to remember whether I had been graded as a child on how much I helped someone else. I remembered that it was part of my conduct evaluation but not part of my education evaluation.

I asked the teacher if conduct was as important as academics in the kindergarten. She said, "The more kind and considerate a child is with his or her comrades, the more he or she is admired and recommended for positions of importance with his or her peers."

After class, the children stood and sang at the top of their small voices to the accompaniment of a piano played by the teacher. The words of the song, in translation, were:

> We are the flowers of our Motherland.
> We grow up in the sun.
> We are the little Red Guards
> We must unite together and welcome foreign guests.
> We must be good little children of Chairman Mao's.
> We are all Chairman Mao's children.

The children applauded at the end of the song, and then we were led into a large assembly room in another part of the school. The doors and windows opened onto a cleared stage area, a piano, and an area where we sat. In the room were the little children we had seen outside wearing rouge and lipstick.

The children put on a show. It was all-singing, all-dancing, and all-Chairman Mao. There was a fifteen-minute play about a girl who comes to school for the first time and loves one toy airplane. As a new girl, she doesn't really understand the theory of Chairman Mao, and wants to reserve the plane all to herself. Gently, her schoolmates educate her about sharing, according to Chairman Mao's teaching of mutual concern for one another. She begins to share the plane, and then all the others begin to share their toys with her. The play ends with all the children playing and reciting: "We must study well and make progress. We should have devotion to others, without considering ourselves."

I took a deep breath, and tried to absorb what I was seeing: the glorification of selflessness, the gentle education of one who does not conform, the refusal to ostracize her, the endorsement of group action, the reverence for the wisdom of Chairman Mao (after a week, even I was referring to him as Chairman Mao). All those strands were present in that little playlet, and everywhere we would go that day, and later, the same virtues were extolled. A child's play, a painting, an opera: all had to make a social point. Essential values were starting to emerge: the elimination of competition and the subordination of individual desires to the common good. It certainly wasn't like playing Monopoly.

In another room, we saw a score of tiny, doll-like children, sitting at long tables and stringing tags that would be attached to sewing machines sold in factories. They were seated at tiny chairs, their hands carefully and intensely manipulating the strings and tying intricate knots. Occasionally a child would look up, but would immediately return to the job at hand. Above the tables was a slogan: "Labor Is Glorious."

We looked at each other, Claudia started to film, and Pat Branson, who was the closest thing to a manual worker among us, was shaking her head. "This is remarkable," she said. "They're teaching these kids the love of *work*, that's what they're doin', and it proves if you start in early enough, you can do it. Remarkable. Remarkable." She paused. "You know, I'm a workin' woman, and I wish someone had taught *me* how to love it."

Then all of us were talking. I heard Margaret say that she thought the children appeared programmed, but Phyllis, who had experience as a child psychologist, objected. "These kids are enjoying themselves, Margaret," she said. "They're learning to be involved in the work force of this society, and that's something we try to *avoid*. We'll do anything to get out of work, but these kids are learning to do more."

"They still looked programmed to me," Margaret said.

Outside, one section of the school was in recess, and almost a hundred children were engaged in a game of tug of war. Some of our American women started choosing sides and shouting encouragement. As if to answer us, the children stopped in the middle of the pulling and chanted to each other, "Friendship first! Competition second! Friendship first! Competition second! We learn from you. You learn from us. We learn from each other!"

The children continued chanting as a teacher looked

on and Claudia and Joan started to film. Suddenly
Margaret leaped into the fray; she chose a side, picked
up the end of the rope, and pulled with all her might
until all the children fell down. The other American
women laughed and applauded, but I noticed that the
children were very confused and the teacher looked
mystified.

The children got up, and the teacher started shifting
the players, so that some of the stronger children would
balance out the sides. She blew a whistle and they started
again. This time, Unita jumped in. She added her 200
pounds to one end of the rope, and managed to topple
as many children as Margaret had.

The class was now completely disrupted, the teacher
was annoyed, and the children were looking at us as if
we were violent and aggressive strangers who had come
to play games to which we did not know the rules. We
had disturbed their game, and we had even applauded
the disturbance. If the lesson of the game really was to
make competition secondary to friendship, we had made
a mess of the lesson. I suggested that it was time to
leave.

Later, as we watched ping pong, gymnastics, basket-
ball, or track, I realized that the same values applied to
all games in China. The object was to excel at the game,
and victory or defeat were irrelevant. In a game like
ping pong, score would be kept, of course, but often it
was simply to measure the accomplishment of the players
and the potential of their own skills. In gymnastics, I
was struck by the tenacity of the children as they tried
to correct their own mistakes. I saw several children
attempt double twists in the air, landing with one leg
on the bar. When they would miss, this was not counted

against them. Instead, they started all over again, trying
until they had succeeded. Whenever a child executed
something difficult, his or her fellow gymnasts would
rush over with congratulations. I thought of a young
boy I knew who had had a nervous breakdown because
he failed to make the Little League team. In China, it
seemed to me, it really did not matter who won or lost,
as Grantland Rice once said, but how you played the
game.

We also visited nurseries, where infants—often as
young as two months—were cared for by state-appointed
registered nurses. Even here, at a preverbal stage,
children were encouraged to share things. Usually,
the children were left at these infant nurseries in the
morning, so that mothers and fathers would be free to
work (some families chose to leave the infants with
grandparents, a task which the older people welcomed).
Almost every factory, commune, or street committee had
such a nursery, usually run by women, "because women
are better with children." Some children were picked
up every evening, others on the weekend, and if a mother
was nursing, she would arrive promptly at lunch time.

The children, dressed in colorful baby buntings, slept
in cribs with mobile toys above their heads, while nurses
(usually one for every three children) circulated through
the rooms. There was a lot of touching, as the nurses
cuddled and fed the children when they were hungry,
and there were toys everywhere: trucks, cars, animals,
spacemen, and balls. The smallest children shared play-
pens with others, learning to touch each other, and on
the day we visited with them, they weren't bothered
by our cameras or lights. They would stop playing for a

few minutes, and then go back with their playmates. I'd never seen a better example of the old saw that to children, we adults are just nostrils.

Here I realized that something tremendously important was happening. I stood in one nursery, watching the children, and I realized that an exaggerated sense of competition was being educated out of China's New Society through its children. From their earliest days, the children were taught to share "selflessly." If children didn't compete over toys, I thought, it would be very hard to compete later for cars or jewelry or homes in the suburbs. It made one wonder if the sense of competition was innate in human nature at all, and because the children seemed so happy and secure I wondered whether mothers and fathers were necessary to children in the same way we believed when their environment was healthy and happy otherwise.

As I watched these children, I also watched the other members of the delegation. There was no way for me to get inside their heads, no way to learn what they were feeling at their deepest levels, and I didn't expect them to react to China the same way I did. But something was getting to them. Claudia and the other members of the crew began to move very slowly. They began to snap at each other. The environment wasn't conducive to good shooting, they said. They began to shoot close-ups of toys. After an hour they looked drained.

On the way back to the hotel, that day, no one spoke. Claudia and Joan sat with their cameras on their laps, staring out of the bus window. All of us, I suppose, were thinking about our own children, or about the way we ourselves had been brought up. I thought about my daughter, Sachi, who was seventeen now, and how

I hoped I had given her a sense of independence. As women, living in a difficult time, we had all struggled with the decisions involved in raising a fellow human being who happened to be a son or daughter, and those who had not might someday have to make those choices too. Yeh and Chang were observing us carefully. I leaned over and asked Phyllis what she thought of it all.

"I'm amazed," she said. "I wouldn't have believed it was possible." She was searching for the words that would sum it up. "Of the children we've seen so far, I haven't seen *one* that I would call even slightly disturbed. It's incredible."

That evening, we all met in Pat's room, to talk over what we had seen. Claudia decided to film the session, which turned out to be as near to the Chinese method of "self-criticism" as we would experience on the trip. We ate with chopsticks, in restrained silence, waiting for someone to begin the discussion. Finally, Claudia, lowered her camera.

"Well, I'm freaked out by what we're seeing," she said. "Those kids have to be programmed to behave the way they do."

"I don't know," Margaret said, shifting from her earlier attitude. "It seems to me they were being taught to share, and that can only be good."

"But all that coddling of the children," Claudia said, "it was freaky."

"What do you mean?" Pat said. "They were getting a lot of attention."

"I don't mean the attention," Claudia shot back. "I mean the jostling."

We were into it. Phyllis pointed out that more often than not the American women were doing the cuddling, "as though the children were dolls." The whole thing was freaky, Claudia insisted. Margaret said that she wished she had been able to send her children to such a nursery when they were small. Phyllis thought the children and the conditioning were both healthy, and the emphasis on work was healthiest of all. Claudia's expression was growing more tense, and she was having difficulty filming us.

"It was freaky, I'm telling you," she repeated suddenly. "I mean, would you *really* want your kids brought up in a nursery? Or a day care center? The truth!"

The room was very quiet. One of the major planks in the women's movement had been the establishment of day care centers that would free women from the drudgery of childcare and housework and allow them to work in the outside world. Now here was a feminist questioning that notion. I asked Claudia if she was upset by the principle of day care centers and nurseries, or by what was going on *in* them in China.

"I'm not upset," she said.

Then what was the matter?

"I'm just wondering why you all feel this way, that's all."

I mentioned the way the women's movement felt about day care centers, and asked Claudia again what she meant.

"Nothing," she said. "I was just trying to provoke the rest of you into exposing yourselves."

Everybody stopped eating then, and Claudia looked like a wounded deer. After a while, we all got up, said good night, and went down the halls to our rooms. China was getting to us. I hoped the trip would hold together, that we would not collapse as so many of the other Western delegations had. As I went to bed, the China I had imagined, with the sands and winds of Karakorum moaning ghostly and mysterious, seemed as inaccessible as ever.

Nineteen

Somewhere near the end of the first week in Canton, I realized how difficult the journey was going to be. Easter arrived with cards and letters from America, full of details about egg hunts and chocolate bunnies, family dinners and back-yard barbecues. Homesickness spread through the delegation like a disease. When our Chinese guides were present, the women said little, but in the privacy of their rooms, it came out.

Pat Branson essentially stopped eating. Her eyes looked like sunken holes and her face took on a haunted quality. Cucumbers three times a day were not enough. She wanted the food she was used to and, in a strange country, could not get. In frustration she would pound the dining-room table for immediate service, knowing that she was not going to eat what she was served, and the Chinese would step back, shocked. When I reminded Pat that she wasn't in Texas, that the Chinese were a proud people and believed that a waiter in a dining room was as important a man as a member of the Central Committee, she calmed down a little, but stayed with the cucumbers.

It was difficult to get angry at Pat. She was punishing herself for all the things that had formed her personality. She was on pills of various kinds: tranquilizers every few hours, stomach-settling pills, sleeping pills at night. Thick with sleeping pills, she would wake up at 4:30 every morning to the jangle of the traveling alarm, in

order to have time to set her two-hour make-up job before her roommate awoke. Unita once told her that
she would be more beautiful without all that make-up,
but Pat said that Unita had never seen her without
the make-up. In all the days we spent together, nobody
ever did.

As the malaise spread, I realized I was consciously
separating myself from the rest of the women. I didn't
want to spend long hours listening to various unhappy
tales. This might be the only opportunity I would have
to see China. I wanted to see everything, taste everything, smell the markets, greet the dawn, stay up late
talking to Chinese about their lives and their hopes
and their struggles. I could talk to Americans when I got
back to America.

But as I separated myself from the others, their unhappiness grew. They complained that Canton was hot
and noisy and they wanted to leave. Ninibah let it be
known that she wanted to leave China altogether. She
told several of the other women, "I'm a stubborn bull-
headed Indian, and when the notion strikes me that I've
had enough, I'll just take off." When I confronted her,
she said she didn't feel that way at all, she wasn't thinking of leaving, she was learning a lot. But it took a con-
frontation for her to say it. So the notion that twelve
of us could join together on a journey of self-exploration
and adventure was rapidly slipping away. We had carried too much baggage with us from America.

Some of the women referred constantly to their
mothers. Margaret didn't, and neither did Rosa or
Phyllis. But Pat and Unita and Ninibah, and the crew,
would talk about how their mothers would react to
China, wondering whether they would eat the food,

what they would think about the way the Chinese
dressed or raised their children, or the de-emphasized
clothes, hair, make-up, and all the other manifestations
of sexual seduction. I suppose, in some way, this meant
that the women were re-evaluating their lives, beginning
with the basic values. I couldn't analyze their motives
but I did know that I was more interested in my own
reaction to China than I was in what my mother would
think about it all.

We might be on a bus, and while I was trying to talk
to Yeh or Chang, I'd hear the others slide into talk
about their boyfriends, husbands, or jobs back home.
Occasionally, they would engage our guides in conversation but more often they talked about America. Gradually I began to understand that the women had never
really left America.

Karen, at twelve, had the least memory baggage to get
rid of. But one day, at a child care center, a curious
thing happened. Karen had made friends with some
young Chinese girls. She picked up one infant, while
holding the hand of a new Chinese friend, and then began to cry.

I wanted to talk to her, and went with her to Claudia's
room when we returned to the hotel. She would have
the freshest, most visceral, most direct feelings about
China, I thought. I asked her if it was all right if we
filmed her reactions to the experience. She nodded, then
broke into tears as the cameras turned. The words poured
out of her. China, she said, was the only place where
she ever had felt safe. In America, she lived with the
door locked, but here, the Chinese were so kind and
sensitive and good that she knew no harm would ever
befall her. She talked about things that had happened

to her in her short life that had caused her to be distrustful of people, and she said she would give anything to stay in China.

She sobbed harder: American schoolkids were cruel because America was a warlike nation; when she tried to work against the Vietnam war, she had been criticized; money and power and ruthlessness were all Americans cared for. But here in China, she "belonged." The tears were pouring, and I held her tight, trying to comfort her.

The cameras ran out of film. Karen's tears subsided, and I walked her to her room, trying to reassure her that things weren't as bad as she thought they were in America, and she should enjoy this trip, learn from it, and go back and tell all of her friends what she had learned. She agreed. I kissed her, and asked her to lie down and rest.

Later that afternoon, she told Pat Branson that more than anything in her life, she wanted to be an actress.

Twenty

In SHANGHAI the Freedom Hotel was large and comfortable, a hold-over from the days when foreigners ruled the city. The rooms had carpets on the floors, thick downy feather beds, and quilts instead of the gray towel bedspreads of Canton. There were bathtubs in which you could lie back and luxuriate. You could walk into the closets, pose in front of the full-length mirrors, touch the white lace on the backs of chairs, and admire the finely chiseled wooden ceiling decorations. The rooms were clean, the linen was white, and we were rejuvenated. We shrieked with delight.

In comparison to the grim functionalism of the hotel in Canton, the eighth floor of the Freedom Hotel was sheer luxury. I enjoyed the luxury, welcomed it, and laughed with the others when someone said that we were just a "bunch of happy capitalists." But I was also relieved because the women seemed happy again. They bubbled as they inspected each other's room, admiring the various views of the great seaport. They rushed to the counter in the lobby and bought stamps and postcards to send home. I went out to look at the city.

Shanghai. I said the word to myself, as I began to walk the streets of that immense city. Shanghai. Fifteen million human beings, all in one place, in a city that was once famous for its exquisite brothels, its opium parlors, its corruption and depravity. I walked along the Bund, that infamous waterfront street where the British had deposited their opium in exchange for Chinese treasures. Here the most notorious prostitutes had once plied their trade alongside their starving countrymen. Now the Hwang Pu was jammed with freighters, tug boats, barges, sampans, and even rowboats. Life was being lived on the river, some of it as timeless as China itself, some of it the result of the great industrial surge of the country since liberation. I breathed in the river smells as the wind whipped my face and I wondered where the Hwang Pu emptied into the mighty Yangtze. I had seen pictures of Mao Tse-tung swimming the Yangtze. I wondered how a man as old as he could be in such good physical shape. I thought of the Long March and the colossal test of human endurance Mao and his band of followers had undertaken. I also thought of the 10,000 people that had been killed by Chiang Kai-shek in 1927. and of how Chou En-lai reportedly had escaped the city by disguising himself as a Buddhist nun. He had headed north to join Mao Tse-tung, knowing finally that in China you couldn't make revolution in the cities. You made it in the Chinese countryside.

I turned into Nanking Road, and found myself in an ocean of bobbing, flowing, bustling humanity. There were bicycles everywhere, and honking vehicles. I saw one teenager take off from "leisure hour" to help direct the traffic; he seemed to have no visible symbol of authority, no uniform, badge, club, or gun; but everyone obeyed his instructions. The whole effect was like some vast human symphony, in which everyone was proudly playing the same instrument.

Shanghai. I said it again to myself. Perhaps here I would begin to understand what their new but ongoing revolution really meant.

That night we ate in the foreigner's dining room on

the sixth floor of the hotel. I wondered what it had been like here in the days before the revolution, when the rich and the mighty ate in these same dining rooms, speaking of power blocs and coprosperity spheres, certain that their empire would last forever, drinking toasts and smiling condescendingly to the Chinese peasants who waited on them. I wondered what they thought then when someone mentioned a small band of revolutionaries fighting somewhere in the hills five days away by foot.

We were served at two huge round tables piled high with chestnuts, spinach and beef, spiced dumplings, beer, and soda. The waiters watched while we ate and giggled and talked over our food. They were very different from the old Warner Brothers portraits of the Chinese. There were no shuffling gaits or obsequious bows, and no potted palms and soft whirring overhead fans making you believe all was right with the world. The food, which was essentially no different from the food in Canton, was good: sweet and sour fish, egg custards, bean curds. We ate with gusto. Pat Branson ate cucumbers.

At·another table, a group of Frenchmen surveyed the food with the amused disdain they reserved for foreigners. A group of Japanese, dressed in business suits, ties, and clean white shirts, represented the new capitalist world. They employed a crisp rudeness to overcome whatever guilt they felt about the Chinese. I talked to the Japanese later, and found them disturbed by China while admiring much of what they had seen. They were clearly threatened by the implications for the future, and I thought about the traffic policeman I had seen in Tokyo tending his small flower before reaching for his gas mask.

There was also a delegation from the British Isles: Englishmen, Welshmen, Scots, and Irish, and because we shared a common language, we compared notes. One thin, red-haired Scotsman complained that he had not been allowed to visit a mental hospital, a complaint that expanded into a tirade against the Chinese.

The dining room became a kind of microcosm, symbolizing the relationships between the foreigners and the Chinese, who now, more than ever, seemed certain that they were citizens of the Chung Kuo, or Central Kingdom, around which the rest of the world revolved. I met a Chinese-American who was shaken by the changes that had taken place since he had left China in 1949. A middle-aged American correspondent, who had been "an old China hand" and was traveling with his wife and daughter, addressed the Chinese with the same condescending tone he must have used when he was young and they were weak. The Chinese were vaguely amused; more than the rest of us, they implied, this man realized how stunning the revolution of China had been.

However, the real China didn't exist on the eighth floor of the Freedom Hotel. It was time to venture into the countryside.

The bus chugged along outside of Shanghai, with the driver blowing his horn at every human being, every chicken, every wandering child, sometimes, it seemed, at every tree. The vehicle with wheels, apparently, was still a novelty in China, and our driver attacked his task with a wild, macho joy.

We passed through village after village, until finally we stopped at a check point where two Red Army men talked to the driver and then let us pass. At this stop I learned that a citizen of China must have permission to go more than fifty miles from his home city. This was like needing a pass to go from New York to East Hampton or from Los Angeles to Santa Barbara.

On the move again, we eventually came to a halt beside a field of waving alfalfa. There we climbed from the bus and lifted our heads to breathe in the fresh clear air.

A dirt road, lined with bushes, led from the paved main road to a small village of baked clay, thatched-roofed homes. This was the Machiao People's Commune. Along the dirt road, people worked in fields of wheat and alfalfa, watering the crops, chatting among themselves under a bright hot sky, applauding and waving to us as we passed. Some stopped their work and simply stared.

A clean open wind was blowing in the countryside. The mindless pollution of China's cities was one of the shocking facts of the trip so far; coal-burning factories spewed dense dirty smoke, the country trains burned coal, and many motor vehicles seemed to burn a raw form of crude oil. It was a matter of priorities, I was told. Meanwhile, it seemed that everybody in China smoked cigarettes, and there was a constant nicotine fog inside hotels and official buildings. But here, the wind was blowing, and the air was dazzling and clean. The women were happy today. Sunshine was a universal tonic.

At the briefing of the revolutionary committee of the People's Commune, we sat at a square wooden table in the main building and were given a statistical sketch of the commune's progress. It had been formed in September 1958, and there were 35,800 people within it, broken down into 8,021 families, 97 production teams, and 20 brigades. The actual labor force numbered 20,824, the

rest being children or old people. The commune produced a varied crop of cotton, fruit, vegetables, oil-
bearing beans, and grain, such as wheat and alfalfa. The
revolutionary committee was evenly composed of men
and women, and they seemed proud of what they had
accomplished.

After the briefing, we walked around the commune
and took photographs. It was almost lunch time, and the
women of the commune were given two hours to prepare
the midday meals in their homes; despite the revolution,
the women still did the cooking. The enticing smells of
soy sauce, bean curd, vegetables, and cooking meat
wafted across the fields.

Here too I began to feel a sense of strength, a common
bond among these people, joined together in a common
task. They were not producing junk to sell for profit in
some second-rate department store. They were feeding
China. It was no small thing to them, and their sense of
pride and purpose was infectious.

In China, we saw evidence everywhere that a real ef-
fort was being made to utilize the skills of women. They
worked on the farms, on the docks, in the factories.
They taught school (which women were not allowed to
do before the revolution), were involved in all aspects of
planning on the revolutionary committees, and were
prominently displayed in propaganda photographs. We
were told many times: Chairman Mao says that "since
women make up half the human race, they must now be
made equal so they can hold up their half of the sky."

But there were no women sitting on the Central Committee. Women were not receiving equal pay for equal
work on the communes. The Chinese worker-peasant is
paid according to a system of work points, which are

allocated on the basis of physical strength and productivity. Since women were usually not as physically strong as men, and took time off because of menstrual periods, their work points were lower. The Chinese themselves were aware of the inequity of such a system. The desire for equality was there, and many Chinese, including many Chinese men, told us that the achievement of equality for women was *the* most important task of the revolution. I found myself less critical of the time it would take to reach that goal in China than I would have been in America, not only because the Chinese attitude was more sincere and more serious, but also because New China had to deal with a past where women had been considered slaves and nonpersons only twenty-three years before.

Girl babies often had been smothered to death simply because they were female and unexploitable as beasts of burden. A wife was literally the property of her husband, and was beaten regularly to keep her in her place. Widows were forbidden to remarry and were stoned to death if they did. The tradition of binding feet imposed such physical restriction on women that they could not walk without assistance. Mental, spiritual, and physical pain seemed to have been the daily regimen of women in Old China, and in some ways the women themselves were as responsible for perpetuating such cruelties as the men. It would have been difficult *not* to buy the mythology of the inferiority of women; Confucius himself said, "Women and slaves are a problem."

So one had to view women's liberation in New China in the context of the total revolution. The Chinese continually reminded us that they were still struggling for total equality: that there was much more to be done, and mainly with the women themselves. A parallel had occurred in America with slaves and women, who often were reluctant to assert themselves because "the white man boss wouldn't like it." Now, however, the men of New China were encouraging the women to believe in their own liberation and equality and seemed to be as involved with the success of "the other half of the sky" as they were with their own. That then was the difference —China was addressing herself to the liberation of all the members of its society through *socialism*, which ultimately meant that people were working for each other rather than for themselves. Once again, I found myself wondering if such a noble and lofty concept would ever really work.

We realized that what we were seeing was almost impossible to film. Claudia and Joan could film women on tractors and show the straight lines of the crops; they could photograph the harvests, with the wheat ready for the threshing mill; take pictures of the barefoot doctors walking country roads, checking children for measles and tonsillitis and a hundred other minor illnesses. We could show all that. We could show the meetings and the young people carefully reciting the statistics that they assumed Westerners always wanted to hear. We could photograph barnyards and babies. We could show the communes equipped with stores, hospitals, nurseries, day care centers, main meeting halls, in addition to the homes of the people themselves. We could show efficiency, both of production and of services provided to the people.

But the truth of China was more elusive. We could not, when all was said and done, photograph the Chinese spirit. We could hardly understand it even

when we were in the midst of it. How could we understand it? We were comfortable middle-class women from
America who had never really suffered starvation and
humiliation. We had not had to sell our daughters as
prostitutes or our sons as slaves. We had not endured
thousands of years of the most degrading human exploitation and oppression known to the human race.
We didn't have to be history scholars to know and sense
what China had been through before her revolution. It
lay behind everything we saw and touched and felt.
China was proud now—of herself and of her potential.
She had pulled herself to dignity and unity and that
spirit literally pervaded the communes, the backbone of
China. The Chinese countryside was where the revolution was won and the countryside was the secret of
China's future.

I looked out across the commune and watched the
peasants and intellectuals working the land together.
The intellectuals had been assigned to the countryside
for a prescribed period of time to work and "learn" from
the peasants. They talked and joked quietly, moving in
and out of the sun. Their body movements spoke of
common hope and common land and common freedom
from hunger and starvation and insult. I did not know
them, they did not know me; we had neither a common
language nor a common history. I wondered about their
common denominator, knowing that I wouldn't last five
minutes down on the farm if I were to be sent there.
Their history, myths, and humor were not my frame of
reference. There was no way to compare what I was
seeing and learning in China to what I knew in America.
I could not live in China, nor did I want to, but I was
happy that we all lived together on the same planet. For

a long time, I hadn't found much about the world to give me hope. But as one day moved into the next, as I watched and learned and absorbed the lessons of China, I slowly found myself able again to hope and trust in the human race.

Twenty-one

THE FUNGCHEN New Workers Residential Area in Shanghai looked like any low-income housing project in any American city, a cluster of plain, four-story buildings set around a courtyard where children played with balls and laundry hung drying in the sun. On the day of our visit, we toured a number of clean, utilitarian flats. We were told that each two-bedroom apartment could house a family of six, with the parents in one bedroom and the children and grandparents in another. These were the homes of the urban workers, the bulk of the 15,000,000 inhabitants of Shanghai whose average salary was $48 a month. One family itemized their expenses for us: rent was $2.50 a month, electricity 50 cents, shoes $2, a suit of clothes $5, medical expenses $2 a year, education $2.50 a year, and food averaged about 20 cents a meal. A radio would cost about $40 and a bicycle $75.

With expenses like that, the families were able to live comfortably. The flats were austere. Portraits of Mao at different ages often hung over bureaus adorned with a vase of fresh-cut flowers, a bowl, and perhaps a radio. Day beds served as couches in the living rooms, and usually there were several hard-back chairs. Illumination was provided by a bare light bulb hanging from the ceiling.

The bedrooms were more personal, with bureaus decorated with children's graduation pictures, family groupings, and sayings of Chairman Mao inserted in the mirrors. The children were responsible for cleaning their rooms, and the men shared all housework, including washing and ironing. However, as in the rural communes, the women still preferred to do the cooking. As Unita saw those neat, inexpensive, clean, and dignified apartments she must have been thinking of the black ghettoes of America, and Pat Branson could not help but make a comparison with working-class conditions, even in white areas, in parts of the American South.

After the official tour, Chang told us that we could wander around at will, and the women fanned out, in twos and threes, to meet some other Chinese families. I asked Chang to introduce me to a family not scheduled on the tour, and she agreed. A few blocks away, we went to the home of a woman factory worker named Liang, who was married and had two children.

Her apartment was immaculate. There were three rooms for nine people, and the furnishings included plastic flowers in a blue vase, a transistor radio, and a table covered with a fine lace cloth. The family served hot tea, hard candies in a bowl, and some small cakes that tasted like a combination of wheat, paper, and a bit of sugar. They seemed flattered and puzzled that a foreign visitor wanted to learn about their lives. The husband was tall and thin, with an outgoing, contagious sense of humor. The son, about eighteen years old, was a tall, gangly kid who kept nervously reaching for a pair of socks that he wasn't wearing under his leather sandals. His sister, a twenty-five-year-old, sat almost primly, with her legs close together. I asked the wife what her life had been like since liberation.

She said she had worked as a young woman in a factory run by the Japanese in Northeast China. The Japanese were cruel and sadistic invaders, and there was a Chinese foreman who was directed to beat her and her fellow workers to make them produce more. She had had her feet bound in the old barbaric tradition at the late age of seven. "My mother did it," she said, "so I would get a husband, which I did." In binding her feet, the toes had had to be broken little by little after they had formed. At the factory, she had to work standing up, twelve hours a day without a rest break, so that by the end of each day her feet were swollen and bleeding. During the evenings, she had to kneel to clean the floor, and that was when the most sadistic beatings occurred.

"But I would rather have been beaten than not work at all," she said. "Two of my children starved to death because there was no food. At least, when I worked I could buy gruel."

Before liberation her husband had observed feudal custom and never allowed her to see or even greet guests. Nor was she allowed to raise her own children because her mother-in-law was the typically cruel mother-in-law of old China. As she put it, "After thirty years of suffering themselves, women waited to revenge themselves on their daughters-in-law." The older women were not permitted to dominate the younger male members of the family but were literally encouraged to do so with the females. Liang also said she had been taught to observe the four virtues:

1. To behave herself according to Chinese morality.
2. To speak to, yet maintain a distance from men.
3. Always to maintain the appearance of seriousness.
4. To work hard and serve as a slave in the family.

As a small girl she had been taught the three obedi-
ences:

1. Before marriage to obey the father.
2. After marriage to obey the husband.
3. In the event of the husband's death, to obey
   her son.

As Liang talked with me, she seemed to regard her
past as a long forgotten event. Chang sat quietly, trans-
lating for both of us. After about an hour Liang smiled
broadly, and asked if I would like to ask Suchu, her husband, about his feelings and experiences since liberation.

When Suchu began to talk, Liang got up from her
chair to sit on the floor near the door.

"This marriage was arranged," said Suchu. "And I
didn't know what I was getting. I had never set eyes on
Liang. She might have had smallpox, or other scars, or
been blind for all I knew. But when I saw her, the day we
were married, it wasn't too bad." Liang laughed, and the
children looked quickly to me to see whether I thought
their father had said something funny.

Suchu repeated the four virtues and the three obedi-
ences and said that because he "observed feudal concepts
in those days," he had expected his wife to obey all
requirements.

"Did you beat your wife in the old days?" I asked,
wondering how he'd react to such a blunt question.

"Certainly," he answered. "Like this." He rose from
his chair, directed Liang to rise too and proceeded to
demonstrate how he used to cuff her around her shoulders and upper chest with his elbows. "All my friends
beat their wives, so I was only observing custom. Sometimes I didn't have any reason except that I hadn't

beaten her recently. Liang submitted to such beatings because she was expected to. Often though, since poverty governed our lives and behavior, I was in a depressed and hostile mood, needing to take my bad feelings out on someone. I didn't really hurt her though, did I, Liang?"

The whole family laughed and Liang shook her finger at him.

I had to ask the question I had waited all my life to ask of someone. "When," I asked, "did you stop beating your wife?"

"Well," he said. "Right after liberation it was difficult for me to adjust to the new teachings of Chairman Mao which forbade me to beat her anymore. I would sometimes lose my temper and raise my elbows to beat her, and she and the children would restrain me, reminding me that Chairman Mao wouldn't permit it, so I refrained. That wasn't easy. I had many talks with my friends who were having the same problems with their wives. The women and children had gotten together to remind us that we had to change. They maintained a spirit of revolt and if we mistreated our wives they would all protest. It was impossible."

"How did you finally change, then?"

"First there were political study groups which taught us that women had to be equal so therefore we shouldn't beat them. Then there was re-education through the street committees and revolutionary committees, but primarily it was through practice. I practiced not abusing her and soon I became aware that she was worthy of being equal."

"Did Liang resist liberation because she had been taught she wasn't worthy of being equal?"

"No, not if it meant I wouldn't beat her." The family

laughed again. "The older women resisted because it meant they could no longer abuse the younger women. Before liberation the older women never did housework. The younger ones were required to do it all. After liberation the older women were required to share the housework along with the men, because if the younger women were equal they were required to leave the home to work."

"How did you feel about your wife going out to work?"

His eyes twinkled and Liang giggled.

"I didn't like it because she was associating with other men. For some time I followed her to work to watch and see what she was doing. But since she was doing nothing and working hard, I felt silly. Soon I wasn't concerned and I stopped following her. I even learned to accept her attendance at the revolutionary committee meetings at night. I realized that if I couldn't adjust to these things with reason instead of jealousy and anger, I would not be a part of the new revolution. My friends, who had also observed feudal attitudes previously, came into a new transition also. We had to, because to do otherwise would be against the law."

Suchu paused and thought. He seemed to be enjoying this oral re-evaluation of his new life with me. He was incredibly open about it, and some neighbors who had joined us were enjoying it as much as he was.

"Sometimes there were arguments after liberation, with the daughters siding with their mothers and the sons with their fathers. We would quarrel. That was the period when self-criticism became useful. I found it difficult at first because I wasn't used to being criticized and would find excuses for my own mistakes. But through discussions with the family and as my political consciousness rose, I felt it become easier. I was then free to criticize others also. Through those free and open sessions we made the transition together. Now it is our new style. The Chinese Communist party under the leadership of our great leader Chairman Mao advocates three styles for the new society: (1) We must combine theory with practice, (2) keep close ties with the masses of people, (3) we must engage in criticism and self-criticism."

"Would you feel comfortable criticizing the state?" I asked.

"Certainly, because the working class is the master of the country. We know we are in control of our own destiny. Then if mistakes are made and recognized we must voice them. Our democracy is a real democracy because it relies on the people. Therefore people can and must take the responsibility of criticizing themselves and others when wrongdoing occurs."

"Do you think your society will change much with the influx of foreigners?"

"Most foreigners only ask questions instead of telling us anything. They don't tell us much how it is in their countries. They usually ask about ours."

"Is there a discernible difference between the ideology of the young and the old?"

"No, except that the young are more energetic. Oh, yes, the young find it easier to adjust to our new society because they never had the experience of the old feudal customs."

"What will happen when your children decide to marry? Will you allow them freedom of choice or will you interfere?"

"We have democracy in our home. We will talk among ourselves. But if either of our children chooses someone we disapprove of, it still would be their decision."

Suchu looked toward his children. They shifted shyly in their chairs.

"Are you planning to marry soon?" I asked the daughter.

"No," she said quietly.

"Do you think you might choose never to marry?"

"No, I have not considered the possibility of never marrying."

I turned toward the son.

"Do you think more girls initiate a relationship now because of liberation? Or do the boys still claim that prerogative?"

He blushed and pulled at his imaginary socks.

"I don't know any girls intimately," he said. "So I can't be sure. But my friends tell me they do."

The whole room burst into laughter and he sank into his chair.

I was beginning to learn that in China personal questions not related to the revolution were greeted with laughter, skepticism, or disinterest. Such questions also seemed to violate the Chinese sense of personal privacy. They were "typically Western" and therefore not "mature." Judging by what Suchu had told me about his own adjustment to the liberation of women, I had to agree with the young people's reluctance to discuss whom or when they would marry.

Twenty-two

No one in China lives alone. As we traveled through the densely populated countryside, or strolled along with massive city crowds, or visited apartments where three generations might share the space, it slowly dawned on me that in China something unusual was happening with regard to sex. For years, I had been an advocate of sexual freedom, feeling that puritanism and sexual repression were essentially political, and ultimately dangerous to all other forms of freedom. In China, some of my most basic beliefs were shaken.

"There *never* was any time for real sexual exploration among the peasants, even before the revolution," Han Suyin had told me before the trip. "They were too preoccupied with the business of survival. Now the nation is involved with building socialism, so the same theory applies."

I was skeptical; sexuality seemed a basic human drive to me, and most psychological studies seemed to bear this out. Then one afternoon, Phyllis and I had a long talk with Chang, our guide, who was a leader in the Women's Federation and had worked, after liberation, in the retraining of China's prostitutes.

According to Chang, the people of China had much work to do, and there was little time to think of things like sex. The state advocated late marriages—at about the age of twenty-six, in order to keep the population down and enable the young people "to devote their good productive years to building socialism."

Chang said that there was practically no premarital sex in China, no prostitution, and no sex education in the schools. "Anyway," Chang said, "by the time the young people reach twenty-six, they know everything. And there is no need to experience sex before marriage. Our young people," she said, "are not attracted by looks or sex appeal, but by political ideology; even if they were attracted to each other sexually, there would be no place for them to go. No place to be private."

There also was the clear association between free sexuality and the exploitation and subjugation of women in preliberation China. To the Chinese a society with free sexuality meant a society in which men took advantage of the women. Chang had worked with thousands of former prostitutes after liberation and knew how difficult it was for them to make lives for themselves. They were unskilled and not many men would marry them.

Chang had been stationed in Norway for a while, working with her husband at the Chinese embassy there. She expressed some curiosity about experimental sexual practices, and even hinted to Phyllis and me that she and her husband had indulged in some of them together. But apparently in China, the conventional "missionary" position, with the man on top, was standard practice, and oral sex was highly unusual. Homosexuality was considered "depraved"; some people told us they had never heard of the practice, while others registered disgust when it was mentioned. Chang also pretended not to understand what masturbation meant, but soon admitted that when little boys were seen doing it they were severely chastised and told they would become "infected and ill." The fear instilled, Chang said, was so effective that the little boys "never did it again." As for girls, she assured us, they never masturbated because they saw what happened to the boys.

Parental nudity in the presence of children was very unusual, and by the time a child was seven or eight years old, he probably would never see his parents without clothes again. It was very unusual for a woman not to marry, and equally unusual for her not to have children. Chang felt that a woman's life would have no purpose without children.

I discovered that ignorance about sex was widespread. One of our younger guides, a pretty nineteen-year-old named Liu Hung, wasn't even sure how "babies were made." In biology class she had heard that "babies grow in the mother's stomach" but she didn't know how they got there. During our bus rides, some of the women in our delegation would rattle on about sex, but Liu never asked questions about what they were discussing. She seemed somewhat embarrassed that twelve-year-old Karen knew more than she did. Liu wasn't alone in her ignorance. Another guide, a thirty-year-old man, consulted his dictionary to look up the meaning of "prostitution." When I asked Chang why the state didn't educate its citizens about sex, she was somewhat defensive.

"The family doesn't consider itself responsible for the dispensing of such information," she said. "The state has officially declared it a private concern. And the schools don't teach sex education."

It was as simple as that. A man and a woman were expected to meet as virgins on their wedding night—with relatively little knowledge of what was expected of them—and work it out naturally. Queen Victoria would have loved modern China.

I could see for myself that in China you were able to forget about sex. There was no commercial exploitation of sex in order to sell soap, perfume, soft drinks, soda pop, or cars. The unisex uniforms also de-emphasized sexuality, and in an interesting way made you concentrate more on the individual character of a Chinese, regardless of his or her physical assets, or lack of them. Someone, somewhere, was having sex, as was proved by the statistics that 18,000,000 human beings were being born in China every year. But sex certainly didn't have highest priority. On a scale of one to ten, it probably rated about number seven.

That was not the case with the American women in our delegation. The feminists talked about feeling "horny" and the others talked about their men with deep longing. There was no possible way to make contact with Chinese men. Later we met American men stationed in China and they described the frustration created by their lack of contact with Chinese women. We all began to miss contact with the opposite sex. Real, underneath, warm human contact. Instead, we found it with the young.

One afternoon in Shanghai, we visited the Children's Palace, a great sprawling structure that had once been a foreign embassy and now served as a massive center for the extracurricular activities of children. A young child was assigned to guide each of us on a tour of the gymnasiums, concert halls, instruction halls, drama workshops, and dance classes. The children held our hands and smiled a lot. They watched Pat Branson going through some of the movements she had learned as a little girl in a Texas dance class, and one of the children

showed Unita a small painting of a black woman with a
baby in her arms. Unita started to cry. "I don't know
what to say," she said. "I don't know what to say. This
is the nicest thing that has ever happened to me." The
little Chinese girl took Unita's hand and moved her
along with us to the next stop.

At the end of the day, we all sat around a long table,
asking questions about the Children's Palace, life in
China, and a lot of other things I don't remember now,
because one at a time, the members of our delegation
began to dissolve into tears. Karen held tight to her new
Chinese friend. Ninibah gave hers a feather. Unita
swayed over the picture. Yeh and Phyllis locked arms,
and Karen buried her head in her friend's shoulder and
began to sob. Tears welled in my eyes. It was as if something tangible—yet mysterious—had touched all of us at
the same moment, some memory of our own families,
some need to regain contact with our own lives. Some
terrible release from the strain of guilt that accompanies
the realization that there are profoundly positive aspects
to the bogeyman called Communism. We became de-
fenseless and raw and vulnerable, and in some ways
resentful that we had been taught to be afraid of it.

That night I wanted to caress and cuddle, stroke and
hold. A child, a dog, another person. That night, I had
one of the two erotic dreams I had in China.

Something even more disturbing was happening to
the delegation . . .

Unita developed water retention in her legs. Nancy
began to run a fever which eventually shot up to 106
degrees. Joan was continually sick to her stomach.
Phyllis coughed a lot and took massive doses of vitamin

C. Rosa fell and sprained her ankle, and Pat's face was beginning to look the color of those cucumbers. Worst of all, Claudia was losing her coordination, stumbling over her equipment. Her hands shook and her lips trembled. I sat with her one day on the bus and asked what was wrong.

"I guess I'm seeing things here that make me analyze myself," she said, her hand trembling as she brushed her hair from her eyes. "I guess I realize how awfully competitive I am, too. I try not to be, because I know how destructive it can be. But I can't help it. Sometimes I worry more about what Joan is shooting than I do about my own work, and I know I shouldn't. We're both good. Why shouldn't there be room for both of us? I even have trouble communicating with her, because I'm so suspicious of my own feelings."

She sighed heavily.

"It'll be all right," she said. "It's just that in China I see all these people working as one person. They're so selfless, and it defies everything I've ever known, personally or in business. It's heavy, you know? That's really what's wrong. If I could stop thinking about myself, I could function better. These people remind me of my own defects, and it's tough to face."

She lapsed into silence and waved me away. I sat quietly, admiring Claudia's raw and vulnerable honesty. She was being affected by China because she was open enough to allow it to affect her. That must be what was happening to everyone, I thought. But it was only the beginning.

Twenty-three ❧

ONE SNOWY NIGHT during the 1972 presidential campaign, I was in a Chinese restaurant in
Milwaukee, and the Chinese-Americans were quite concerned about what was happening on the TV set. They
should have been. On the screen an American president
named Richard Nixon stepped out of an airplane,
walked on Chinese soil, and was greeted by Communist
Premier Chou En-lai. The Chinese in the wilds of the
province called Wisconsin were astonished.

Now we were in Peking, stepping out on that same
tarmac where Richard Nixon had been greeted by Premier Chou En-lai. This time the representatives of the
Communist party of the People's Republic of China
were all women. They were waiting for us on the other
side of the entrance fence, and greeted us with outstretched hands and warm embraces. Behind them the
airport terminal rose like a masculine statement of
official policy. A portrait of Mao Tse-tung stretched
across a hundred feet, looking down on all the new arrivals. At the top of the steps leading to the terminal,
two Western men seemed to be staring anxiously at us.
As we came closer they stepped forward.

"Jim Pringle and Jonathan Sharp here," one of them
said. "We're from Reuters news service and we thought
you'd like to hear about Shui Men."

"Shui Men?" I asked. "What's that?"

"Water Gate," Pringle said, and then they handed

me pages of wire service copy. "Shui means water, and Men means big gate, and it sure does look big."

We leafed through the copy. Haldeman and Ehrlichman and Kleindienst had resigned. John Dean had been fired. All the flimsy dams that had been constructed against Watergate during the Nixon campaign had burst now, and the whole corrupt mess was pouring out. The women looked at each other. Pat Branson, her face red, yelled, "All right, all right, I'll never vote for a guy like that again!" Unita was jumping up and down and Margaret said, "I might be a Republican, but I *am* from Massachusetts."

Our Chinese hosts didn't understand. I stood there staring at the wire copy as it flapped in the Chinese wind, in the capital of the People's Republic, on the far side of the earth, and I remembered McGovern's wounded face when so much invective was hurled at him because he was too decent to fire Tom Eagleton. One of our guides looked at me with a puzzled expression.

"It's the man who calls himself our president," I tried to explain. "He's been caught with his hand in the cookie jar."

"Oh, yes, Mr. Nixon," she said. "We were pleased and happy to have him here."

There was no way to explain, and I didn't pursue it. We walked to the bus that was to take us to the Minzu Hotel.

There were long lines of poplar trees on the avenue leading into Peking, and lines of people riding bicycles, their bells making a gentle, tinkling sound. Something struck me as odd—and then I realized there were no dogs. Not on the broad main boulevards or the side streets of the old preliberation Peking, with their teeming markets, busy citizenry, and dusty building sites. Not a dog in sight. I asked my guide why.

"They weren't useful to the revolution," she said, with a flicker of a smile. "So they were allowed to starve, or were eaten."

I fought down the temptation to make a wisecrack about running dogs, or Pekingese. And then a long black limousine moved past the bus, shiny as diplomacy itself, and the window rolled down. A handsome African dressed in a Western business suit leaned out and shouted: "Hello, sister! Welcome to Peking!" Unita rolled her window down and shouted back: "Yes, sir, I knew I liked this place! Yes sir!"

We all laughed. Pat leaned over and yelled, "Well you gottcha one, Unita—he's all yours."

The Chinese called the Minzu Hotel the hotel of the "nationalities." It had housed the press during the Nixon visit, and now handled much of the growing stream of foreign visitors. After the comparative luxury of Shanghai, we were back to revolutionary functionalism: tiny rooms, grimy tubs, temperamental toilets. But there was something new here. Peking is just south of the Gobi Desert, and in April and May the wind blows steadily, bringing a thin fine layer of dust and powdered sand that sticks to your hair and skin and makes it hard to breathe without coughing. I hoped this would not make our visit even more difficult than it had been in the other cities.

I didn't need to worry. Not about dust. When we arrived, we discovered that the ninth floor of the Minzu Hotel housed the crew of the new communications

satellite facility that was being built in Peking. The crew
was a mixture of Americans, Australians, and Englishmen, and they hadn't seen a Western woman in months.
Our adventure into China took a decided shift.

The remainder of our journey together was spent in
Peking, and the ninth floor became a refuge for most of
the women—from loneliness, from culture shock, from
the strange New Society that they were seeing every day.
The Western men had been there for six months, and
although they admired most of what they saw, they
couldn't wait to leave. They wanted to see "women's
frills and other feminine things," as one of them put it.
If they were in China, they wanted to see the old Suzie
Wong *cheongsam*, with the slit up the side, and complained, with only a hint of shame about being such
blatant male chauvinists, that "women's equality" had
created "unisex" clothing that made women drab and
unattractive. Some of our women seemed to agree.

After a few days the ninth floor started to look like a
coed army barracks. A short-wave radio blasted country
and western music until the Chinese attendants looked
as if their eyes would cross. There were a lot of bawdy
jokes about "chinks" and laundry men, and after most
of the women would leave at night to go to bed, the
sound of heavy drinking and carousing continued for
hours. The arrival of our group of "female women," with
make-up, earrings, colorful clothes, and a gift for flirta-
tion, had turned on the men of the satellite crew.

During the day some of the women dutifully made
trips to the more obvious tourist sites, other women began to stay in their rooms. The dust became thicker.
Colds and coughs grew worse. A few women stayed up
most of the night drinking with the satellite guys, so they

were too exhausted in the morning to see China. Ninibah called her boyfriend and asked him to ask *her* to come home, as if that would release her from the responsibility of fleeing on her own. He refused, telling her she was having the experience of a lifetime and she should stay to the end. Unita discovered several men from Zambia who were studying at Peking University, and would entertain them until three in the morning; her edema grew worse, and Margaret would spend hours massaging Unita's legs. Unita then felt so guilty that she could not ask Margaret to close the open window, and ended up with a deep chest cold. Nancy's throat was so sore she could not talk. Joan's fever led to a diagnosis of pneumonia, and she had to be hospitalized. Karen made friends with several children her own age, attached to the Canadian embassy, and soon spent most of her time swimming with them.

I couldn't believe what was happening around me. I was continually apologizing to the Chinese about our behavior. One member of the delegation locked another out of the room they shared, and so we needed two rooms. Rosa wanted meals without pork. Cabell wanted corn bread and slowly dissolved into tears one day as she was recording sound at the Institute for Minorities Studies. The loneliness of the minorities made her homesick, she said, and she couldn't control herself. Karen started acting impolite to anyone she considered a "servant." Joan insisted on leaving the hospital, and the Chinese released her with reluctance, telling her that she must have bed rest. Claudia was having dizzy spells, and when Joan returned to work, the friction between them increased. Margaret was openly angry at the other women for acting like "a bunch of spoiled children," and in a more subtle way Phyllis tried to persuade them to control themselves. Nothing worked.

Every journey in which more than one person takes part becomes "Rashomon," and I suppose each of the women would have a different version of what actually happened in Peking. At night I asked myself over and over if it was my fault, whether I had picked the wrong women, whether there was anything more I should be doing to make things easier for them.

I had thought I was a democratic and sensitive leader when I first undertook the adventure and would be able to handle any trouble because of that. I soon realized that I cared more about what I was learning and seeing than I did about the problems of the women. China was something I had looked forward to all of my adult life and I found myself disregarding anything that short-circuited the realization of that dream.

Unita had asked for a "gripe session," which might have served the same purpose as a Chinese "self-criticism session," but I was afraid that the group would blow apart, that we would scream and shout and say unforgiveable things to each other as we honestly verbalized what was on our minds.

I suppose most of what happened had to do with the fact that we were Americans of a certain generation, inculcated with the belief that Communism is bad. Yet in China, we saw low food prices, and streets free of crime and dope peddling. Mao Tse-tung was a leader who seemed genuinely loved, people had great hopes for the future, women had little need or even desire for such superficial things as frilly clothes and make-up, children loved work and were self-reliant. Relationships seemed free of jealousy and infidelity because monogamy was the law of the land and hardly anyone strayed. All of these things, so different from what we were accustomed to in America, shook us in ways that left us no conventional response. We could not write a card that said, "Having Wonderful Time, Wish You Were Here," because ours wasn't that kind of trip. It was a quantum leap into the future, and for some of the women, the prospect must have been chilling.

As my sympathy for the women warred with my anger at their lack of self-control, I became more and more determined not to get sick or depressed myself. When I felt a sniffle coming on, I willed it away. If something upset me, I concentrated on a shaft of sunlight or a distant waterfall until the moment passed. I had never used my will in quite this way before, not in any film, not when I danced, not in any personal relationship. And in the process, I must have matured ten years. I couldn't have known that in a few weeks I would lose control too.

I went out and embraced China, seeing performances of *The Red Detachment of Women*, a splendid revolutionary opera with a solemn social message which was compensated for by great beauty of production and the forceful discipline of the dancing. Karen skipped this for a showing of *Butch Cassidy and the Sundance Kid* at the Canadian embassy.

Some members of the delegation visited the Forbidden City and the Great Hall of the People on the same day. The Forbidden City was both intricate and opulent, calling up images of the emperors of China, with their many wives and concubines and servants. The Great Hall of the People was massive and solid, built by the rulers of the new China, dedicated it seemed, to confidence in the people. In the meeting halls were thousands of seats, and I had the impression that decisions in the Great Hall would take as long as it took the delegates to be heard. I thought back to our Democratic convention. Was it possible to have two kinds of democracy? One in a dictatorship, and the other where there is almost no leadership at all? There were square meeting rooms on each floor, representing each minority group in China with arts and crafts and paintings depicting each autonomous region. More than anything else, the Great Hall of the People symbolized the personality of the New Society. Pat missed that visit. She stayed at the hotel making posters for a birthday party for one of the satellite men.

On May Day we sat as honored foreign guests in T'ien-an Men Square, on a day of brilliant sunshine, watching dancing and singing typical of various regions throughout China. Hundreds of scarlet flags billowed in the breeze. There were military ballets depicting the revolution and it was difficult to tell whether the performers were soldiers who had learned how to dance or dancers who had learned how to shoot. In each ballet, the "soldier people" were overthrowing the past. I thought about the Russian celebrations of May Day I had seen on television, with long lines of tanks and rockets and marching infantry, and I thought of the supermilitary parade I'd seen at Nixon's inauguration. I had expected the same display of military prowess in China, but aside from recalling the revolutionary past, the military aspects were not emphasized. Fathers held their children on their shoulders, and young people photographed each other in the great square, and everybody seemed to be eating popsicles. As legions of young people welcomed their foreign guests, they seemed to

be one massive, curious face. It was a feeling I had
everywhere I went in China. I never had the impression
that 800,000,000 *individuals* lived in China, although I
knew this to be true. The prevailing impression was of a
unified colossal presence.

The music and dancing lasted for hours, and then an
older Chinese woman sat down beside me. Immediately
she was surrounded by photographers and admiring on-
lookers. The woman's face was majestic and kind, her
eyes full of mischief. She wore a plain gray Mao suit.
Because of her bearing I realized that she was Someone
Important, but I didn't know who. I asked and then
learned to my embarrassment that she was Teng Ying-
ch'ao, the wife of Premier Chou En-lai. This woman had
been through it all; she had fought on the Long March
with her husband, from the beginning of that epic 6,000-
mile retreat in 1935, to its end. She had seen her com-
panions die on the roads and in the hills of China. She
had handled a machine gun herself and had contracted
tuberculosis fighting for the new vision of China. Now
she was here beside me, and I didn't know what to say.

So I listened as she talked, asking about what *we* were
like and how *we* were enjoying China. I told her I was
sorry I hadn't recognized her. She said it wasn't important because *she* wasn't important. She said both of us
were only important insofar as we could help to make
the world a better place. She congratulated the delegation for representing the American women.

Later, in a meeting over orange soda and nuts, I asked
Madame Chou En-lai about the role of the artist in
China. As though she anticipated my question, she
admitted immediately that the New Society had to
provide a more conducive environment for artists, writers,
and intellectuals, but expressed the need for state con-

trol of art and literature. When I told her that I, as an artist, could never accept state control of creative expression, she nodded and said she understood but went on to explain softly, almost gently, that when you have a country whose major problem is feeding its millions, art and literature must play a secondary role, and then only to serve the interests of the revolution. She said there was no essential difference between art and politics in serving a new nation and that the *people* were the highest priority. She repeated that she and other leaders recognized the need to give artists the opportunity for creativity—because ultimately without this the progress of the revolution itself could be hindered.

I wanted to question her about Chiang Ch'ing and Chinese writers and the need for criticism. I wanted to know whether she agreed that art and individuality helped make people more human while politics helped make humans better organized. But her gentility and the clarity of her explanation made me hesitate. Perhaps if I had been Chinese I would have pursued my questioning. But coming as I did from an entirely different frame of reference in the West and from a past that was privileged rather than deprived, I let the moment pass and enjoyed the orange soda and nuts.

When we said our good-bys three hours later, our women cried. Madame Chou En-lai cried too. Dabbing at her eyes with a white handkerchief, she waved us on to enjoy the rest of May Day and kissed each woman good-by. I wished Unita could have met her. She had been with her Zambian friends the night before, and was too tired to come.

One morning about seven, Margaret heard Pat Branson fumbling in the bathroom and went in to see what

was the matter. Pat was vomiting blood. Margaret called
me and I called the doctors, who arrived almost immediately. Pat had bleeding ulcers, they said, and there was
only one treatment at this point: soups, soft food, and
bed. Pat blanched. She had had ulcer attacks at home,
and had not had a drink in five years. However, the
night before, in the barracks on the ninth floor, she had
stayed up late drinking vodka.

"I didn't come to China to stay in bed," she said,
lying back like a sad, skinny bird with paint on its face.
"I'm just lyin' here, gettin' weaker and weaker. I'm just
gonna get worse."

She crawled from the bed, went to the bathroom, and
vomited more blood.

"You see?" she said. "It's not good for me to stay in
bed."

I didn't know what to say. Pat was hurt; she didn't
need temperance lectures from me. But she stayed in
bed that day, and when I went to visit her, she started to
tell me about her life, about growing up in Port Arthur
with parents who "dressed me like a sexy little doll and
then wouldn't let me go out with boys." There had been
a first unhappy marriage, a lot of bad jobs in terrible
places, and a second marriage that was better. She now
talked with a kind of gut-level honesty, knowing that
somehow she had not often played fair with herself. Before she went to sleep, she pulled out her diary.

"Look, Shirley," she said. "I've been writing down
some of the thoughts of Chairman Mao. He's said some
beautiful things, you know, and I want to take them
back to the people of Port Arthur, Texas, so they'll
understand that he isn't saying anything much different
than Jesus Christ."

Well. I asked her if she was certain she wanted to do that.

"Sure, Shirley," she said. "Why, I'm gonna take back the Little Red Book, too . . . They have a lot of good quotes about organization in there. We have to learn to organize in America. That's our problem—no organization. If we *don't* organize, the Communists are certainly gonna come and take the country away from us."

Twenty-four

ON THE DAY we were to visit the Great Wall of China, Claudia appeared in the lobby, dressed in a mini-dress with a plunging neckline, and high straw lifts. She was wearing lipstick and mascara. China and the Western men had apparently gotten to her. Until then, the crew had worked in coveralls and flats or sneakers. I didn't care about the make-up, but it seemed absurd to try to lug a twenty-five-pound camera and fifty pounds of film up the Great Wall in a miniskirt and high heels, and I told her that. Claudia went back to her room and changed, but something in her seemed to want to break out.

At the Great Wall, we saw people from all over the world—Arabs, Frenchmen, Mexicans, Japanese, and a lot of Chinese, on holiday or days off from work. There were small knots of Red Guards and People's Liberation Army silently watching the foreigners, and Ninibah gave them something to remember. She went right to the wall, sat on a ledge, and started to beat her Navaho drum, singing a native song to the mountains about the beauty of nature. The Chinese blinked. Foreigners were very strange and demonstrative people. I noticed that for the first time during the trip, Ninibah looked happy.

The clear day, and the clean wind combined with the surrounding mountains and trees seemed to relax everybody, including Yeh, the guide who had been with us from the beginning. She started to talk openly about her own life, not caring about the camera, telling us that even at home, the goals of the New Society were subject to different interpretations. For instance, "My husband tries his best to wash and iron but he doesn't do it well," she said smiling. "So it's necessary for me to do it again." She worried whether she had "the proper attitude" toward understanding the needs of her baby girl, and explained that what had attracted her to her husband was "political ideology." When I said that everyone in China seemed to have the same ideology, and therefore she could have married *anyone,* she smiled in amusement at my Western logic. She said there was a more important priority in China than *who* you married.

"We marry to have children," she said. "We hope those children will be good little red soldiers who will help to spread Chairman Mao's thoughts to all those who are oppressed. My husband and I work together for that, and we are very busy. We want to have a better life, more understanding, and we are striving to be self-reliant and selfless. We want to carry out the teachings of Chairman Mao."

On paper the words seem those of a robot, but Yeh was hardly a robot. She had a nice sense of humor and a warm human quality to her intelligence. Our questions about marriage, children, and sex seemed rather odd to her (some of the Chinese thought we were "sex-obsessed), because she lived in a world where people worked from six to six, and spent evenings at political meetings or in self-criticism sessions. Children were regarded as participants in the revolution rather than possessions of an individual family.

"Individual preferences are always discussed," she said,

"but the preferences never become deviation, because our spirit is one of collectivization. All personal problems and preferences are solvable and possible through the thoughts of Chairman Mao. "What is best for the masses," he teaches, "is best for the individual." When people are unified, it doesn't matter much whom they marry as long as the mutual love shared is for the sake of unity above all else. The love for one another flows from that." She paused for a moment. "One chopstick can be broken," she said. "But massed chopsticks are impossible to crack."

As she talked, I noticed that she was holding Phyllis's hand.

Time was running out now, and we were on our final round of visits. We saw a baby delivered by Caesarian section with acupuncture as the sole anesthetic. Joan got dizzy during the operation and had to lie down, but overcame her squeamishness and continued to film. During the operation the patient, whose stomach was surgically exposed, ate an apple and waved to us.

We saw a factory where deaf mutes, more than four hundred of them, worked busily making machine tools. They were organized into their own revolutionary committees, held self-criticism sessions in sign language, and some were undergoing acupuncture treatment for deafness.

I asked to see a film studio but somehow that never worked out. There was nothing being filmed, someone said, but I sensed that the Chinese simply didn't want to be observed working at this medium until they had decided where it fit into the society. The Chinese were always honest but hesitant whenever I asked about writers or artists or filmmakers. This might have been because they knew this was my field in the Western world, and knew I would report knowledgeably on what I found. I also felt though that the role of the artist genuinely confused them in their New Society. They hadn't yet figured out what to do about artistic revolutionary democracy in a society where the spirit of the collective was all-important. I sympathized with them. So far as I knew, no one had been able to figure that one out.

As we moved from school to neighborhood, from briefing to briefing, I had a growing feeling that the Chinese way might be the way of the future. Then I remembered what had happened to the intellectuals who had visited the Soviet Union in the 1920s and 1930s— Lincoln Steffens saying, "I have seen the future and it works"—and the disillusion later when the word filtered through about the death camps and Stalin's murders and people who disappeared in the night.

Certainly we were seeing carefully selected places; the Chinese obviously were going to show us their best, not their worst. But there was none of the paranoia that seemed to infect the Soviet Union; the Chinese spoke openly to us, without looking over their shoulders, and the sense of unity seemed to come from the bottom up, from that peasant and that factory worker who had acquired a sense of dignity and worth in the years since his liberation from the past. I never felt that the unity of China was being imposed from the top down, or through the use of terror.

But I still hadn't seen enough. I wanted to travel into Yenan, to the birthplace of the revolution, to see what kind of countryside and life had forged that remarkable group of men and women who had made the revolution.

However, the growing problems with our delegation were making that difficult. The women looked progressively more haunted, as they absorbed each insight, started to make the step into understanding, and then retreated. At the briefings and other sessions, they seemed closed in, as if what they were learning had made them numb.

I had applied for an extension to our visas on the day we had arrived in China, knowing that the China Travel Service in Peking would need time to check their transportation and housing facilities, and also to decide how they felt about us. At first the women had been enthusiastic about the possibility of a longer stay. But that was in the first great flush, when some of them were giving interviews about the wonders of China two days after arriving. Now they seemed to be shell-shocked. I didn't pursue the extension for the full delegation, but asked if I could stay a little longer on my own. The travel agency agreed, and the other members of the delegation acted for once as a collective, sighing with relief.

All except Phyllis. Two days before we were scheduled to leave, even Phyllis gave in. She came down with pneumonia and was taken off to a hospital.

The rest of us were on a train staring out at the countryside, trying to comprehend what was happening.

I looked over at Pat. She was dabbing at her eyes. Gently sliding in next to her, I asked what was wrong.

"It's what I'm seeing," she said. "It's the people—they're so happy. They have so much less than we do but they act so serene and peaceful. I wish I could find out why. I wish I could know their secret." Big tears welled in her eyes and she held her stomach.

"We're missing something in our life, Shirley . . . I'll tell you that, and these people aren't . . . If only I could find out why."

The mood was somber on the last day in Peking. The doors of the ninth-floor rooms hung open and empty, with old copies of *China Pictorial* on the bureaus and some discarded package wrapping and pieces of wire copy lying around on the beds. The satellite guys came to say good-by, looking glum and abandoned, knowing they would have to struggle on now with each other. Pat moved around, saying good-by and giving out her Texas souvenirs to the puzzled Chinese. She touched me in some very special way, because of all of us, she was the only one who was giving something back to the Chinese.

Yeh and some other officials came down the steps of the Minzu to say good-by, asking us to bring their greetings to the American people. And then Yeh got on the bus with us, and we went to the airport. The women didn't look back.

At Peking Airport we waited for the plane to Canton, where they would get the train to Hong Kong. The women talked about what they had seen. They would miss the mole on Chairman Mao's chin; the experience was the most important of their lives; the Chinese had done a wonderful job with their revolution. They placed women's liberation pins on the jackets of the women guides. And then we boarded the plane for Canton. The women talked now about clean air and Hong Kong shopping and boyfriends and Honolulu, and Pat Branson smiled. At last, there were no tears.

Yeh and Chang came with us, and when we landed

at Canton, in the middle of a torrential storm, they took us to an airport hotel, where we would spend the night. In the morning we would board the train for the border, after which I would return to Peking. As we walked into the hotel, Joan collapsed, pale and trembling, her face ashen.

"I'm all right," she said. "I don't have a fever. I'm all right. Don't make me seem sick. I'm all right. I'm just tired."

I took her temperature and it was 106 degrees. She didn't want a doctor but we called the hospital anyway. Yes, the doctors said, they expected her to get ill again. They had a report from the hospital in Peking, and if Joan did not go to the Canton hospital, she would be seriously ill. I pleaded with her, but Joan didn't want to go.

"No, no," she said. "They'll tell me I have to stay there."

We pleaded with her, bargained with her, and finally got her to the hospital, where x-rays showed a large spot on her right lung. She sat on the edge of an examination table, paste-white and vacant-eyed, her face twisted in defiance.

"I am not staying in this hospital," she said to Chang and Yeh. "I'll leave this country tomorrow if I have to drag myself across the border."

The two guides, who had been through so much with us over so many miles that they seemed a part of the delegation, stood there, faces blanching. I took them outside, and apologized, explaining that Joan was sick and feverish and didn't know what she was saying. Chang and Yeh smiled weakly. I went back to Joan.

She had promised that if her x-rays showed a spot she would stay.

"If I stay in China," she said, "I want another American with me."

I asked Margaret if she would stay, and she said she would be delighted to see more of Canton. The Chinese extended her visa, and I traveled with the others to the border. I remembered how much promise there had been only a few weeks before, as we traveled these same tracks into China. Now most of the women were leaving like stragglers from a demoralized army. Joan was in a hospital, with Margaret in attendance. Phyllis was in a hospital in Peking. The others were subdued and silent. At the customs shed, Unita tried to lead some singing, choosing the old songs of the civil rights movement, but her attempt seemed hollow. I twisted my ankle doing a Mexican hat dance. Nothing worked. A group of Chinese customs clerks, all women, looked on as we danced, then joined in, laughing. But the dancing and singing ended as soon as the train to Hong Kong was announced. One by one the women came to me for hugs and good-bys, and then rushed to the train, moving past the sign that said, "Long Live the Unity of the People of the World."

The train started, its wheels squealing against the metal tracks, and then it was gone, and I was alone.

In Canton, Joan had calmed down, responding to the gentle care of the Chinese, a good book, and the kindness of Margaret. She apologized for her behavior, and said she had only been angry at herself for getting sick. She promised that she would not leave the hospital until

she was better. I said good-by to her and Margaret, and
went back to Peking with Yeh and Chang.

All the way back, I thought of a conversation I had
had once with Han Suyin, who warned me that I might
have trouble with a delegation of women. Men had an
easier time in China, she said, because men respond to
matters of economics, industrialization, profit and loss,
gross national product, and the like. But women relate
more to the fundamental revolution in human values
that has occurred in China, particularly if there are no
men present to neutralize the shock. The real changes
in China involved the way children were reared, the
values of kindness, mutual respect and need, notions
about work and the home and how to get along with
your fellow human being. These were usually considered
"lesser" feminine concerns in Western societies, but here
in China they were the primary concerns of everybody.
In a complicated way the women on the delegation were
to be complimented for being sensitive enough to have
been affected by the fundamental changes to which they
had been exposed.

That was part of what had gone wrong, and it was too
much for all of the women, including me. China was so
fundamentally different from our way of life that there
was no easy way to identify with it. My sinuses were
clogging now, and despite some medication I'd taken
in Canton, I was starting to sniffle. It didn't matter. The
women were happy to leave China, and at that moment,
alone in the Chinese airplane, with the country sliding
beneath me at 500 miles an hour, I was happy they were
gone.

Twenty-five 🌸

PHYLLIS WAS WEAK, and still bedridden, and the Chinese said she would have to stay in the hospital at least another week. So with Chang and a battered suitcase, I started across China by train, heading for the Western provinces where the revolution had been born.

The country was spread out around us, wild and harsh and primitive, and I began for the first time to understand that the Chinese Revolution had very primitive roots. Here was a country in which weather, landscape, wind, and climate had conspired against people. And people had fought to overcome nature for centuries, and then were forced to fight other people, until now the Chinese realized that their only real friends were each other. They were the only people who were in permanent alliance against their brutally dry countryside, and their strength came from each other.

The train smelled of ginger and lilacs as we sped along. My mind tossed with ideas and insights, some as flinty and hard as the landscape we were passing through. After almost a month in China, everything was up for examination. The notion of freedom was suddenly suspect; in American terms, there were no freedoms here of the variety we cherished: no freedom to publish, no opposition political parties, no freedom to write books or create works of art. But there were other freedoms: freedom from starvation, discrimination, exploitation, slavery, and early death.

I found myself thinking with such broad strokes in China. Human nature itself seemed increasingly relative to me. I had grown up, like many people in the West, believing that human nature was composed of a number of permanent concepts: competition, the joy of ownership, acquisition of land, aggressiveness, jealousy, selfishness, the need for self-expression. Every single one of those concepts was standing on its head here. People seemed content, even happy. I don't mean deliriously happy. That had not happened anywhere in human history. But these people were content, living in a kind of theocracy that included a godhead (Mao), a creed (the red book), and a belief in the ultimate will and justice of the masses. And what bound it all together was faith.

It must have required incredible faith to decide to struggle against the harsh land we saw from the train. Dust blew everywhere, swirling over dry caked mountains, coming in under the windowsills of the train, and still people worked, tilling wheat fields, carrying buckets by hand, moving continuously in the dust storms. I saw terraces hacked from the stone faces of mountains, with row after row of crops planted in dirt that had been carried up the mountains by hand. There were caves dug out of the faces of cliffs, cool in summer, warm in winter, a tribute to endurance in all seasons. Slogans were splashed in red paint against the cliffs.

ASK THE MOUNTAINS TO BOW DOWN
    THEIR HEADS
LET THE RIVERS GIVE WAY
LET THE CROPS GROW FROM BARREN LAND
FIGHT AGAINST THE SKY
FIGHT AGAINST THE EARTH

Everywhere the struggle was active, allowing no room for despair, free of the debilitating religious passivity that was killing India, or the greed that was beginning to strangle America. At some point a man came on the train and with Chang as interpreter asked whether it was true that in America the farmers had killed two million chickens to force up the prices in the markets. Yes, I said, it was true. He shook his head in disbelief. He came from China, where the soil had been tilled longer than in any country on the earth, and where food was a precious thing. He did not believe that a civilized country would kill chickens unless they were to be eaten later. There was no way for me to explain it to him, then, or ever.

I looked out the window, at farmers in straw hats walking home now in the dusk, and saw another poster, in Chinese, which Chang translated for me. It said.

SEIZE THE DAY!
SEIZE THE HOUR!
ONE DAY IS EQUIVALENT TO TWENTY YEARS!

We moved through Yang Fen, Yang Chuan, Han Suin, and across the Wei River into the province of Shensi. The train left a thick slash of black soot on the clean horizon. And we couldn't open the window because of it. A man came through spraying ginger and lilac scent again, and when I asked why they allowed the pollution from the train, he said: "We have no other resource."

The man accepted the pollution. Things were better than in the past. And he sprayed some of the perfume into the slowly whirring fan, which gently circulated it through the compartment.

I sat thinking of China's indifference to the environment. I had seen it everywhere; in the black smoke belching from factories, in the sludge that accumulated in the river beds near factories. Factories seemed to be China's highest priority. *Man must conquer nature through industry.* Industrialization was everything. Progress was industrialization and vice versa.

A Chinese-American friend of mine had described an afternoon he spent with old friends who proudly showed him a successful textile factory, and, as proof of its achievement, pointed out the now dormant river which no longer flowed because it was so thick with industrial waste.

The blindness to the problem was astonishing and the need to *overcome* nature was all-encompassing. I knew that northern China had a traditionally hostile environment, which had produced a sense of fear in the humans who lived there; their natural inclination was to conquer nature, not amalgamate with it, but I wondered where it would end. Would the skies and rivers of China finally become so polluted that the Chinese would take action? Or would they continue their blind pursuit of their original revolutionary plan to industrialize before all else?

The train pulled into Sian. As Chang and I stepped down I was dazzled by the brilliance of two huge crimson flower vases spilling with blossoms and greenery. Bursts of flowers dripped from windowsills everywhere. I was overcome by the profusion of color in this country where hard work and self-discipline are the overwhelming priorities. I looked around me. I was almost 600 miles from Peking. Had Mao's revolution really spread this far? Was the ancient Chinese capital of some 500 years ago as involved with the New Society as Peking had been?

Chang and I walked along the street. I could hear natural sounds: a bird's whistle, trees combed by the wind, the rustling of flowers, a child laughing somewhere. All around us, along the breezy, tree-lined streets, people were working. Most were dressed in the traditional revolutionary garb. Some women wore jade studs in their ears, and there were a few teenage girls in brightly colored silk blouses. People pulled carts of fruits and vegetables in the old way, like beasts of burden. I asked Chang about this.

"Change takes time," she said. "It will be some time before we bring technology to central China. But these people have learned to be proud of their back-breaking work. They know it is different now, because they are doing the work for themselves, and not for the landlords." Even though we saw echoes of the past, the revolution was in Sian too.

Chang and I were met by two members of the Sian Bureau of the China Travel Service who took us to a hotel with empty echoing halls. There we were given separate rooms. I was in a small suite, and Chang was somewhere in another wing. I had hoped that we could room together, so that I would have time to get to know Chang better, without the group conditions that had prevailed when the American women were part of the journey. However, even at dinner time we were separated; she ate in one place, and I ate in another. The first night I sat at a table alone, eating shredded beef and peppers, water chestnuts and mushrooms, steamed buns, chicken broccoli, rice and fresh oranges, and I was disappointed. I wanted company. *Chinese* company. I had been in China long enough, I felt, to establish more personal and intimate contact with Chang. Apparently the rules decreed otherwise. Or perhaps it was a cultural preference on the part of the Chinese themselves.

Most of the other foreigners I met in China were disturbed and disappointed by the lack of contact too. We were told that it was not the "authorities" who ordered the separation; the Chinese guides and the Chinese people did not feel comfortable with outsiders, a feeling that seemed to have its origin in the recesses of Chinese history. It was as if they realized how difficult the adjustment to China would be for so many of us, how brimming over we were with questions that they might not be able to answer. It was easier to maintain space between us.

I retired to my room and sat on the windowsill, looking out over the garden while an orange moon rose behind the rustling pine trees. I was overwhelmed with a sense of strangeness, a sense that my world was different now. Something had happened to me that I did not understand. Here in this hollow hotel, with its orange Chinese moon, all the old assumptions were subject to question and all the old rules relatively silly. The moon did not seem to be circling the same planet that housed Pinewood Studios, the Howard Johnson's Motor Lodge in New Hampshire, or the make-up room at MGM. And the next morning, when I visited the Panpo Museum, built in 1958 over the archaeological remains of a Chinese civilization that was 6000 years old, I was even more discombobulated. These ruins had been unearthed six feet below the surface, and despite the age of the land and the ruins, the Chinese guides insisted on explaining that forgotten civilization in terms of Mao's China.

They claimed that the civilization was communal, which might indeed have been true, but there was simply no visible evidence to support such a theory. I saw a deep ditch surrounding the ruins, to protect the inhabitants from wild animals, and there was a storage bin for human waste materials and garbage. The guides claimed the bin was communal, and therefore there were no social classes in ancient China. At death, each person was buried with three relics, and this was supposed to prove that there was no private ownership of goods.

Each family obviously lived privately; even I could see that. And each home was separated from the next by a circular mound of earth. The guides told us that the Sian ruins were from a matriarchal society, in which women were the principal organizers because they were better acquainted with planting, farming, and other agricultural tasks, while their men hunted for meat. The surviving artifacts, which the guides said were made by women, were advanced and imaginative; birds and animals sculpted on clay, paintings made on the sides of homes, on pottery, shells, and bark, and there were a number of examples of bracelets and earrings, evidence of a society that had time for matters beyond mere survival.

"Practice makes art," one guide said, relating these artifacts to modern China. "Science and art and knowledge come from practice. The people with the most patience are the most capable. And this civilization proved that."

Again, I was struck by the contradictions. On one

level, Mao Tse-tung was clearly saying that there was
no such thing as human nature, that man could make
of himself whatever he wanted to make. On the other
hand, the guides were trying to stress the correctness of
Mao's revolution by giving it origins in civilization that
preceded written history. To me it didn't seem necessary to impose a history on those ruins. The best proof
of Mao's theories was the modern Chinese people
themselves.

I walked around the ruins, wondering about human
nature, about all the pop theories of the past few
years, from the territorial imperative to the basic sav-
agery of the human heart. I hadn't seen any examples
of hostility in China since the Cultural Revolution, not
even a simple quarrel between bus driver and passenger,
and it slowly dawned on me that perhaps human beings
could really be taught almost anything, that perhaps we
were simply blank pages upon which our characters are
written by parents, schools, churches, and the society
itself. If evil and fear and oppression could be written
on those blank pages, then so could kindness, sincerity,
goodness, compassion, and a collective spirit. I wondered which human truth was true. In fact I wondered
what "truth" meant. I was beginning to question whether
positive change might not be more important than
"truth." Perhaps truth was nothing but education. And
if the education was progressive and positive maybe it
was worth the compromise of the "reinterpretation" of
"the truth." The Chinese seemed to feel that truth was
nothing more than what they believed it to be anyway.
Was the same thing true in the West?

I had spent a lot of my life feeling lonely in the "individualistic West," but here, in this "collective place,"

where I knew neither the language nor the people, I was not lonely. I almost felt at home. And I hadn't smoked a cigarette in five weeks.

In the next few days in Sian, I looked at more relics of the ancient past, visited abandoned pagodas (to the amusement of my hosts), and met with a revolutionary committee, which differed from its Shanghai and Peking counterparts only in the nuances of dialect. The message was the same. The revolution *was* life to the Chinese.

When we could, Chang and I would also discuss America, and I would try to explain my feelings, talking about what had gone wrong, about our obsession with military power and the disparity between rich and poor, and the continuing struggle everyone was making toward true equality. I admitted that sometimes I plunged into despair.

"You must believe in the American people," Chang said to me one day, in a rather sweet tone. "They will soon rise up and overthrow your imperialist government that suppresses them."

Her naiveté was amusing, and she was so sure, that I didn't know how to answer her.

On the day I left Sian to take the plane to Yenan, I saw a crowd of thousands of young people in the early morning mist, waving paper streamers and playing drums and musical instruments. I asked Chang what was going on.

"They're seeing off their young comrades who have been assigned to work in the countryside," she said cheerfully. "They are responding to the call of Chairman Mao to integrate. A good revolutionary citizen is one who is willing to integrate with workers, peasants, and soldiers."

The young people were laughing and singing songs as we drove past. Then, observing that I was a foreigner, they broke into applause. I waved, and the applause grew, a spontaneous display of friendship and affection from these thousands of smiling young people. I glanced at Chang.

"You see?" she said. "You must have patience. The people will do the right thing."

The applause faded as I waved back and we drove on. I realized that my eyes were wet and I was breathing hard and sighing deeply.

Twenty-six ✿

THE APPROACH to the Yenan airfield was like a trough, with mountains rising steeply on three sides. The mountains, sliced, terraced, and planted by Eighth Route Army revolutionary hands, were monuments to the perseverance of man. Yenan was the birthplace of the Chinese Revolution, the place where Mao Tse-tung and Chou En-lai ended the Long March and located the base camp for their Eighth Route Army. Here the New Society was born. Here the revolutionaries scooped caves in the mountains and ate grass and melted snow in order to stay alive.

As we dropped straight down, I realized why Mao and Chou had chosen this place forty years before when they and the Chinese Revolution were young. Yenan was easy to defend. Among these mighty mountains, the Eighth Route Army had taken the worst battering from the Japanese and Chiang Kai-shek—and had survived.

The past assailed and enveloped me as I walked for the first time through the streets of Yenan. The people had their own special hard character, with flat, resilient mountain faces. There was a mountain look to the homes and the layout of the streets. Mao's personality seemed to pervade the place—in the sun-baked caves where he had lived with his army, in the rough soldier's architecture of the assembly hall his men built, in the dusty wind itself as it blew down from the mountains past lookout posts where sentries had kept watch and past all the thousands who still worked with their backs and their hands in the fields.

But the most special thing about Yenan was its simplicity. Clean and spare and simple. It was the sort of place where Mao Tse-tung must have reduced his ideas to simplicity itself, where he must have examined the writings of Marx and Engels and taken from them what he felt was best for China, discarding the rest. It was a place where the winters must have been brutal, driving him to the warmth of the caves, where he and the others could plan a society in which no child would die of hunger, no daughters would be sold to brothels and no sons sold as slaves, where no person would ever again bow before another. It was a place where he must have made hard decisions about himself, and those decisions forged a personality of such resilience, discipline, and foresight that he changed the course of the lives of one quarter of the human race. His vision, like Yenan itself, had a kind of harsh purity.

Now, some thirty years later, Yean is haunted by its own revolutionary spirit. Its people are proud that they were present at the beginning. I could see peasants toiling in the harsh wind and sun, their small children following and learning firsthand the continual lesson of survival. The baked dusty mountains rose like palisades. I couldn't conceive how people got to the top, but they did—bringing soil and water by hand in order to plant crops. Dust swirled in small circles around me.

Along the village streets, some people stared at me; others hid when I came into sight, and still others walked directly up to me to look into the strange blue of my strange round eyes. A few asked questions I couldn't understand. Sometimes Chang was with me and acted as interpreter. A boy of about ten asked if I was a foreigner. I said I was and he said I didn't look like the other foreigner he had seen. Who was that? A Japanese. He had once seen a Japanese. A spunky old woman hobbled on bound feet and stopped in front of me. She looked closely into my face, her jade earrings dangling.

"Who are you?" she asked as Chang translated. I laughed. Her ancient eyes flashed as she demanded to know what I was laughing at. She was proud, curious, and defiant.

A schoolboy wanted to know if I had ever been to Peking. I nodded.

"Have you seen Chairman Mao, then?" I shook my head. No. He went back to reading a revolutionary comic book and walked away.

One day, on a mountain road, a group of families from hillside cave dwellings overlooking the town invited me to spend a day with them. Their lives were both communal and private. One woman was the leader of the community. I felt as though we were long-time friends because there was so little tension between us. The men discussed their adjustments to the liberation of women with me, although some were reluctant to talk about life before liberation. The past seemed to make them anxious and unhappy. But generally, the men were humorous and made jokes about how their women managed everything—the finances, the organization of the community, and the raising of the children too!

The women showed me how they baked eggs in clay ovens beneath their caves. They showed me photographs of their children and letters received from them after they had been assigned to the countryside farms. One young girl had just returned, and stated she found the two-year experience difficult but illuminating.

"It was good for me," she said. "Now I want to become a doctor."

I met some housewives who had organized themselves into a communal sewing group to repair and make clothes for all in the immediate vicinity. Did they receive money for their work?

"A little," one of them said, "but as long as we have two hands we feel we should help each other and the revolution."

Another group of housewives had recently formed their own revolutionary committee and had just elected their officers.

"We need to help with activities for our children. For the time being we are concerning ourselves with that task."

Still another group had opened a noodle shop. They mixed their own flour and water into noodles to augment the diet of the peasants outside of Yenan.

I talked with people about religion, death, marriage, money, and happiness, and all the while I was trying to figure out their New Society.

I left the cave dwellings and noticed I was having difficulty breathing. My nose and throat felt clogged. I couldn't see three feet ahead of me. The dust of Yenan was blowing into a fierce storm, settling over the entire area.

I stumbled ahead, feeling as though I'd rather not breathe than take the dust into my lungs. I tossed my head from side to side. But there was nothing to be done. The clean mountain air had *become* dust.

At my rest house hotel I spent hours in the warmth of the bathtub, thinking about China. I wasn't a philosopher, but Yenan was forcing me to think with more clarity about what I had seen. I had so many questions. How did the intellectuals who had been assigned to the countryside really feel about being "re-educated by the workers, peasants, and soldiers"? What could a plow-wielding peasant actually teach a Shanghai poet after the novelty of the first few weeks was over? Sometimes intellectuals were required to stay in the countryside for years. Was this de-emphasis of the elite a good thing? Did it help equalize the entire society, or did it abort intellectual creativity? Should *anyone* be considered special in a society where *everyone* was considered equal? The questions came in waves, but I really didn't have answers yet.

Why did the Chinese seem to be so much happier than the Russians? Both countries were born in socialist revolutions, and paid allegiance to the thought of Karl Marx. Yet when I visited with the Russians in the 1960s, they seemed fearful, depressed, and suspicious, while the Chinese around me were trusting, open, and vital. Was it a simple difference in national characteristics, or was it differing interpretations of Marxism? I thought I had understood what the word "revolution" meant before coming to China, but after being there awhile I realized it is a word of many meanings. To the Chinese the word is a symbol for ongoing change. Revolution in China never ends, because life is a continual struggle. Mao, the Chinese say, didn't make revolution to gain power, but gained power in order to make revolution. And that revolution dealt with everything in Chinese life from economics and agriculture to how people related to one another. The Cultural Revolution took place under the umbrella of the ongoing revolution. Whatever its details meant (and I spent a great deal of time learning and asking about it), the Cultural Revolution was only a part of the scenario for human change that was the task of the next twenty years in China.

As I reflected on this vast human experiment I wondered why the Chinese were able to accomplish so much in such a short period of time, and this led to even more painful questions. Was it because dictatorships can move with more speed than democracies? The Chinese proudly used Lenin's phrase "the dictatorship of the proletariat" to describe their political system. But there were dictatorships—of the proletariat or otherwise—all over the world, from Franco's Spain to the Soviet Union, and they hadn't come close to the human success I was seeing in China. There was something else going on here. People related to each other in a way that I had never seen before. And as I moved around I became more and more convinced that it was because of a technique called "the self-criticism session." I didn't know of any foreigners who had seen such sessions, but I had spoken about them to many Chinese people, including Ambassador Chou Huang-Hua and Deputy Foreign Minister Chou Kwan-Hua.

The self-criticism session is conducted at every level of Chinese life. The familial level, revolutionary committee level, university level, factory level, middle school level. From what I could discover, most of the 800,000,000 Chinese, including the Central Committee and Mao Tse-tung himself, participate in self-criticism a few times a week. During the sessions each person tells the others what he thinks of them as well as what he thinks of himself. The prevailing attitude is usually open and honest, but also kind and considerate. As a result of such open and direct communication—even though much of it is extremely painful—there is evidently a marked decrease in frustration, hostility, repressed emotions, and fear. Since there is continuity in self-criticism and therefore a constant examination of values and attitudes, people tend to act as watch dogs on their own behavior, taking care not to slip back into habits of unkindness, selfishness, or noncommunication. The self-criticism sessions then became more and more easy to tolerate because attitudes of kindness and consideration improve.

I thought of how such a session would go over in America. The real purpose of self-criticism sessions in China was to keep the leadership honest. It did not matter whether the leaders in question were on a community or national level. In fact, the most important sessions of all revolved around the behavior of duly elected officials. Apparently the honesty demanded by the people was excruciating. I wondered how our politicians would stand up in sessions like that.

In New China the most crucial change was that demanded of the men, because they were being asked to give up nearly all of their traditional values regarding private ownership of land, exploitation of slaves for money, the subjugation of women, and complete authority over their children. Somehow the Chinese man seemed to be making the transition, because he knew it was necessary for the ultimate success of the revolution. Besides, Chairman Mao had decreed that he must.

I lay in the tub wondering how I would react to a self-criticism session, when I found it hard enough to talk to just *one* doctor in a therapy session. I was sure

I'd find myself wanting to figure things out privately, or wanting to write something, or dance or act in a way that would express the feelings that I found difficult to communicate otherwise.

Then I began to speculate on the effect that self-criticism in China might be having on individual creative expression. Perhaps honest group communication reduced the need for individualistic artistic expression in the New Society. Since so many human creative forces are based on a desperate need to communicate one's feelings, perhaps the need is displaced in a society that practices intercommunicative therapy. In that case, perhaps I wasn't seeing a censored artistic community, but rather a community that simply had no need to express itself in art. I had talked to many artistic people—writers, filmmakers, dancers, and directors. I had no way of knowing whether they told me the truth, but all seemed to feel they were currently living through a transition period—a creative and artistic pause which would help facilitate a more important goal if they applied their creative abilities to the revolution rather than pursuing individual artistic needs and desires. The purpose of art and literature was to serve the people and the revolution *now*. Later on—who knew? Would there even *be* art and literature later on? And would anybody miss it?

I sloshed around in the tub, adding more hot water; and thinking about America. I thought of America's climate of anger, violence, crime, and corruption, of her selfishness and deception, and her freewheeling abuse of freedom. Yet I not only had to live in America, I wanted to. I could never live in China, that much I knew. And it wasn't possible to believe that a phenomenon like the Long March could be accomplished in America. It would be impossible for a group of Americans to establish an American Yenan somewhere in the Rockies and descend later as a revolutionary army of the future.

Still, revolution had happened once in America—with Jefferson and Thomas Paine and Patrick Henry and George Washington. Perhaps it could happen again? Did the experience mean that it is never too late to change values capable of turning us into monsters?

Yenan made me contemplate the world in apocalyptic terms. It made me embrace hope as a realistic possibility, because I saw how a small band of "believers" had turned human nature inside out. Once again I felt that human nature was what one decided to make it. I considered my own nature. Why was I so attracted to the collective way of life when, above all, I wanted to reserve my right to be an individual? Was I still unwilling to give up those extensions of myself that made me wealthy? Was I as much a slave to possessions and money and the good silken life as those I had accused in the past? Was I as much a packet of contradictions as I seemed?

If it hadn't been for the comforting, warm water in the tub in Yenan, I think my mind, will, and resistance would have crumbled. I felt as though my spirit and soul had been turned inside out. China was finally getting to me.

One afternoon, Chang asked a "responsible member" of a local revolutionary committee to see me in my room. She was a middle-aged woman and her name was Tam Lin Po. She sat on the couch in my room, with her sandalled feet crossed, and spoke in a soft, hesitant voice about her past and all the bitter past of China. Chang translated.

"My grandfather was a poor peasant," she said. "He

had no food for his family. During the famine of 1929 he was afraid his family wouldn't survive the harsh winter. His brother had joined the Kuomintang forces and had money and surplus grain. My grandfather asked him for some survival grain for the winter, which he would pay back in the spring. His brother refused. My grandfather was desperate so he asked some other male relatives for help. They went to the brother's house and stole some grain—not much—but enough to carry them through a few weeks.

"When the brother discovered the grain was missing, he questioned my grandfather. Grandfather admitted taking it, saying he had no choice. The next day the Kuomintang arrested my grandfather and the other relatives involved. They were shot. So all the women in the family were widows. My mother was pregnant with me at the time. In old China it was customary never to allow the widow to bear a child in the home of her husband if the husband had died. My mother was forced to leave her husband's house and give birth to me in the fields outside the village. Widows were never allowed to remarry so she took me to another village where she was unknown. Two months later she married another peasant so that she would have a place to live. He died of scarlet fever because he couldn't afford medicine.

"We lived on wild herbs which we collected along the mountain ridge. Sometimes my mother would lock me in our hut because she was too weak to lift me when we walked. I couldn't walk well anyway, because my bones had no calcium. Sometimes we had millet but when I saw my image in the bowl I knew it was only water. Our hut had no full roof and when I lay on the floor at night I could see the stars. When it rained, our hut was a river of mud inside. I was always miserable, always cold, and always hungry. I never laughed and became very sullen. My mother taught me to spin when I was older but it didn't help much.

"When I was about ten I heard about something called a school where the landlord's children went. They said that people learned to read and write there. I went with my friends to see what it looked like. We climbed the stairs to the entrance and a teacher saw us. She screamed at us and called us filthy pigs. Then the students and teachers came out of the school rooms and beat us. We tried to run but we were too weak. They left us bloody until finally we were able to move and leave.

"When I was twelve my mother married another poor peasant, because two people could eke out a living more easily than one. My mother had another child—another girl. At first they considered letting her die because girl babies in old China were worthless, but they decided to let her live.

"Then one day two friends came and told us about the Red Army. They said the Red Army was liberating certain areas where poor peasants such as we lived. They said the Red Army wanted to help the people. They said the Red Army had a camp and that if we went there they would help us.

"We packed the few belongings we had and began to walk. We came to a border patrol where the Kuomintang officers were standing guard. They asked us where we were going. We told them we were going to visit relatives. They said they would let us pass if we gave them something. We offered them whatever we had. They became furious when they saw we had nothing and bayoneted my mother's arms and threw our belongings over the side of the mountain. Then they beat my father. The more he pleaded for mercy, the more they beat him. I stood very still, hoping they wouldn't harm my sister and me. I was afraid that they would take my father and force him to be a member of the Kuomintang because they used to force men into their army. But my father was too weak. They didn't want him. They let us pass.

"We walked for six days and six nights. We couldn't stop because we were afraid we would be found and arrested. My father carried us on his shoulders. That is when I slept. On the sixth day we heard singing in the distance. I asked my mother what the singing was about. I had never heard many people singing before. She squeezed my hand and told me to be quiet. I wanted to run toward the happy sound but she told me not to be happy or I might be punished. When we walked closer we saw people working together in the fields. Then we saw the soldiers of the Red Army working with the people.

"I asked mother again what was happening because I could sense something different in the air. Then five Red Army men came toward us. They took us by the hand, gave us food right away, and said we were welcome. I had never had that kind of experience. I asked my mother if it was safe to be happy now or would they punish us. She smiled. I had never seen my mother smile like that. 'It's Chairman Mao,' she said, 'and the liberated area. We are safe now.'

"The people in the base camps were friendly and immediately collected food, clothing, and some furniture for us. They gave us a place to live and some land. It was the first land we had ever had. The first year was difficult because of the weather. But the second year produced crops.

"At fifteen I went to my first school. I didn't know anything, so I had to catch up. I worked every night studying over an oil lamp, because we didn't have electricity then. I was ashamed to be in a school with children six years old but I began to get very good marks. I studied for two years very diligently and soon I made such good marks they sent me to a teachers school. In 1946, with the Civil War raging, our school moved wherever the Red Army moved. I became an active revolutionary and did propaganda work. I worked with the masses on land reform. From 1947 to 1949 the struggle was difficult in Shensi Province because the area kept changing hands. But the Red Army worked closely with the people.

"My task was to mobilize women to help make shoes for the army. I went into one of the villages secretly to mobilize help. The Kuomintang spotted me. I was visiting an old woman who knew everyone in the area. The Kuomintang broke into her home and tried to take me away. She screamed that I was her daughter. She didn't even know who I was working for, but she grabbed me and wouldn't let them take me. They bayoneted her arms, but still she wouldn't give me up. She intimidated the Kuomintang until they went away. I left soon afterward so I wouldn't involve her anymore. That old woman saved my life and I still think of her today as my other mother. During those times the best and the worst in people came out.

"I worked hard with the Red Army and today I lead a happy life. My mother had another child. I have two children myself who are also in the army. I never found the rest of my relatives. I hope they are leading happy lives. I owe everything to Chairman Mao and the Chinese Communist party. Not only my family but thousands and thousands of families in Yenan would have died without his leadership. Now I'm a responsible person and a leader in my district. I am a leading woman and it's important that I remember my bitter past. I should respond by working hard to do a better job and because of my happy life now I should guard against arrogance.

"We had a saying when I lived my previous life. 'The rich were like the top half of the sky—their wealth was never ending and the poor were like the bottom half that rains—our tears were never ending.' My life has been no harder than hundreds and thousands of others but we now have a new life and I will dedicate mine to it."

Tam Lin Po wiped the tears from her eyes. I looked out the window, at the dark dust, and felt ashamed.

The warm bathtub became my consolation and refuge. I couldn't eat because dust was in the food. I began to feel claustrophobic. What would *I* have been like, I wondered, in those early Chinese revolutionary days of the 1930s? I was strong and resilient and someone had once called me "a guerrilla traveler." I had survived a coup d'état in Bhutan, lived with the Masai in Africa, and traipsed across India alone, but China was another matter. It is a nation that forces you to face yourself, and I wasn't sure I liked what I faced. I fell asleep with my window closed tight, but it didn't help. In the morning, my face was coated with a fine layer of dust.

I woke up coughing. My watch said nine o'clock but

it looked like early evening outside, and I couldn't see the tree outside the window. Dust hung in the air and slowly powdered everything. I felt trapped, almost as though I were a prisoner of my own dramatic visions. I wanted to think things through to a conclusion. I also wanted to leave Yenan, in order to alleviate the pressure. But there was no plane, and there would not be one so long as the dust held; I knew that.

Stumbling down to Chang's room I asked if we could somehow get a car and drive away from Yenan.

"It wouldn't be safe," she said. "The driver couldn't see either. Besides, the roads are nearly impassable. You must have patience." Her brown eyes expressed sad annoyance. Why couldn't I accept the circumstances? Why was I so compulsive and irritable? It would only make things worse. I could see that she considered me another spoiled American woman. Yes, China had really gotten to me, and I was not handling the experience with any more grace than the rest of the delegation had.

The morning was the color of rust. I knew the sun was hanging somewhere beyond the dust but I couldn't see it. I walked through the village again, by myself. After our talk, Chang instinctively understood I wanted to be alone. I had told her how my beliefs and values were in turmoil; that I was seeing that it was possible somehow to reform human beings and here they were being educated toward a loving communal spirit through a kind of totalitarian benevolence. She knew how I felt about totalitarianism. We had discussed it many times. But that was the big lesson of China, and it left me immobile. I just didn't want to believe it. Not in my American heart. Not in my American bones. Yet I as one who aspired to art and the supreme importance of

fan, eating a kilo of fresh lichee nuts, sweet and cool and sensuous. We met two Canadian embassy men in a restaurant, and grew slowly aware again that sex existed in the real world, not simply in dreams. But we were drained, emotionally and physically, and only cared about the cool breeze wafting off the Pearl River and the children who were swimming in its clear water.

The train to the border was crowded with foreigners, including reporters who wanted my personal impressions of China. I couldn't tell them. I didn't try. They talked about a press conference in Hong Kong and I said sure, knowing that I would never do it. And then, very suddenly, and very easily, China was behind me.

The approach to Hong Kong was raucous and loud and smelly, filled with exiled Chinese hustling jade and girly magazines and their sisters. We passed huts squashed into filthy piles, polluted ponds, and stops where elegant Chinese women in *cheongsams* stood next to beggars with skinny bodies and dusty skin. Faces turned toward us, as if we might bring some news that would make life more bearable, as if New China could rub off on them from us who had traveled there.

Among the skyscrapers and hustlers of Hong Kong friends whisked us to a waiting car. Reporters jammed microphones in our faces and asked for a minute of instant profundity. I could not talk.

We went to the Hilton, where I could see a turquoise swimming pool from the twelfth-floor room, where my feet dug into the deep nap of the carpet, where I saw an American sailor on another floor throw a whiskey bottle into the pool. I smelled chocolate, and delicate fruit, and turned to the coffee table, where baskets were wrapped in cellophane. Two mints lay on the pillows of the interior-decorated bedroom. Free cologne and perfume rested on the sink, and there were fluffy white terrycloth robes, with matching towels, for our use. Room boys in white jackets arrived with drinks, and backed out with their hands extended. I took a bath. And wondered which me had been in that little tub in the hard mountain town of Yenan and whether the dust had returned.

We went to dinner in the glass-enclosed restaurant on the top floor of the Hilton, where Western men and women eyed each other's newly acquired bargains. Fingers flashed with diamonds and pearls. Precious stones adorned chests and moved when the women breathed. There were a lot of hastily cut silk suits too. The sound of violins caressed the air in the candle-lit dining room, where the tables were heavy with bowls of iced vegetables, cut-crystal wine glasses, bowls of fruit and nuts. Businessmen consumed martinis and joked with the higher-priced prostitutes. A few unescorted women sat alone, waiting for whatever the night would bring.

I ordered roast beef, dimly aware that my friends were talking about vegetarianism. The wine steward hovered behind me, with a gold taster hanging from a velvet cord around his neck, and poured three separate wines into three separate glasses for me. I was handed a Caesar salad in a teak bowl on a silver tray. A man with a proud, almost arrogant face came by with a cart filled with bread and decorated with roses. The roast beef arrived, pink and succulent-looking, with fresh grated horseradish beside it, and I was presented with a silver platter from which I could choose any of twelve vegetables and five varieties of potatoes.

I picked up the knife and fork, and they felt clumsy
and barbaric. I cut into the meat and felt a sudden
twinge of nausea. I began to chew and then the plate
before me was swimming in circular motions, the color
of the vegetables blending with the wine and the table
cloth. As politely as possible, I got up and tried to glide
to the ladies' room. Two tears splashed into my butter. I
said I'd be right back.

As soon as I closed the door of the cubicle, I knew it
would take a while. And then I started to cry. I didn't
really know why, but it had something to do with all
those people in a place called America, all those faces I
had seen in crowds and in the living rooms, all the be-
trayed and insulted people I had seen in black ghettoes
and white factories who felt they were essentially worthless. It had something to do with them, and the women
on my delegation and their confusing human hang-ups,
and it had something to do with George McGovern
coming across those two hard years, to see it all go wrong
at the very end. It was about him, and about the cookie
jar in my mother's kitchen, and the white pigeons in the
yard, and the people who were going to jail because they
were forced to be criminals, and the families who couldn't
make the payments that month on their cars and their
mortgages. It was about Sheldon Leonard, who didn't
want to do it the hard way anymore, and money-made
art, and Lew Grade who believed everybody had a price,
and all the frightened, talented artists of Hollywood,
selling their homes and reading the trades, waiting for
the call that never came and wanting to be loved more
than anything. It was about Mankiewicz and Hart and
nights on press buses on lonely country roads, and about
afternoons in the fresh snow of New Hampshire, and

the good exhausted feeling that morning in Miami when
we thought we would change the world. I was spent, and
I cried for a long time, and didn't care what anyone
thought. I really didn't care at all. I was going home.
In fear and hope. I just wondered if I could get there
from here

Epilogue

I spent the following year trying to understand what I had seen, felt, smelled, touched, and sensed on that trip to the other side of the earth with a group of American women. The experience of China was unlike anything else that had ever happened to me. I could add up the days, the hours, the feelings, and the places, but the sum came nowhere near its total effect. China was a case of the facts having very little to do with the truth.

People who had gone to China with other Western delegations had had the same problem; an inability to articulate what they had seen on the same emotional level as they had experienced it; a frustrating failure to communicate what the experience does to one's own basic values. In so many ways the experience of China is tearing and painful, but that is because it is self-revealing.

Each of us on the delegation had come from different social and economic backgrounds, and if I hadn't been trying to represent a fair cross section of American women, we probably never would have come in contact with one another so intensely in the first place. So we were not only journeying through China, but through one another, and ultimately through ourselves.

"Listen, Shirley," said Unita, "I understand what's going on over there in that China because they're peasants and that's kind of what I come from over here and what they've got going over there is fantastic. I mean, it's disgraceful over here. You're afraid all the time someone's looking over your shoulder, can't go on the streets at night, young ones on dope. I learned about our value system, in China, honey. I mean the things we care about. Even in the civil rights movement we been caring about a lot of the wrong things. I mean, our system over here always wanting more *things*. It's gonna collapse on top of us; we just can't make it with what we're doing. I know we acted like asses over there sometimes, but it was because of what we realized."

I asked her what she meant.

"I mean caring about what clothes we wear and what cars we have and what trinkets and all that," she said. "I understand now that what they're doing is important because they care about each other. Even with that, my mother was worried, you know, because they don't believe in God over there. But I said to her, 'Well, they got their own sense of God.' I tell her it looks to me like God is people. An' she seems to understand that. She really does.

"My friends say I'm more peaceful and happy," Unita told me. "And I guess, deep down I am. That agony of trying to be better than somebody else was getting me down. I don't care about that anymore. Things you *do* are what's important, not what you have. Like looking at the buds on my window sill. And you know the best part? I thought this new feeling would fly away someplace. But it hasn't."

When Ninibah Crawford returned from China she sold her trailer, bought a small house in Tuba City, switched to another job on the Navaho reservation, and got married, not necessarily in that order. She said that the China journey had made her look more closely at her own identity.

"America's system fits the needs of the white middle

class," she said. "But not my needs. Sometimes I wish America had been discovered by a Chinese Communist Columbus. Maybe then the Indians wouldn't have been slaughtered. The Chinese at least allow their minorities some self-identity. So I suppose, in some way, China helped me reinstate my old values. Values which made me a more unified part of my people, as compared to the values I was taught by outsiders. Remember the Navahos have no word for "communism" because it basically describes our way of life. And when I saw how much freedom the Chinese give their children, I realized I was holding my teenagers on too tight a leash. The tighter I held, the more they wanted to get away. I've changed. Now I let them go, and we're both happier. Personally, I'm more self-assured. I feel confident about expressing things that might not be popular, and I don't feel as threatened by the truth anymore."

Pat Branson—who had never been away from home before, who had confidently explained to me once that Henry Kissinger had to be a Communist because he once worked for Nelson Rockefeller—had hit the lecture circuit since returning to Texas, and was explaining to one and all how Mao Tse-tung and Jesus Christ were brothers under the skin.

Pat Branson was the only member of the delegation who came from the white working class. She worked for a large corporation, and depended on that paycheck every week. She did not challenge the system that employed her, but understood it enough to realize that the only way to defend herself against it was to organize. She was a strong union member, and worked hard in local Democratic politics. She gave her allegiance to

George Wallace because she felt that the Democratic party was falling into the hands of people who didn't understand her: the educated, urban "intellectuals." Unita and Ninibah were members of minority groups organized in the name of a cause called justice, but Pat hoped for more money and fairness from the system. What had affected Pat the most was China's ability to organize.

"The women, the children, they're all organized into jobs," she said. "All my friends around here are interested in that. They don't ask Communist questions at all, and my God, I been speakin' everywhere. I'm booked all through next year. They ask me what impressed me the most, and I tell 'em the way people are working together to build up a country.

"Some people wanna know if they tried to enslave me over there, or brainwash me. I put it to 'em this way, Shirley. I say these Chinese believe in Chairman Mao's teachings and I say if that's what they want to believe in, great. Because what they had twenty-three years ago was pitiful. Ol' Mao, he gives 'em something to look forward to. Maybe they did show us only the pretty things, but if they came to our country, we'd do the same. We sure wouldn't show them the slums and things like that. I tell them nothin' changed me into bein' a Communist but, well, I do have a different outlook on life.

"You know, I appreciate what I've got here at home so much more than I did. I realize how important it is for me to have a job like I do and how lucky I am to have a country like this to live in. I'm going back to work in politics and organize to help clean up some of this dirty stuff underneath the table. It's pitiful what those corrupt politicians are doing to us. I saw the Chinese take a stand for what they believe in. We could do the same thing. People here sit back and let everyone else do the work. The Chinese don't do that. They're involved. If somethin' is wrong, they fix it. I think we should all read that Little Red Book so we can learn *how* to organize; otherwise, like I said before, we're gonna be taken over by the Communists."

Pat talked on in a rush, with passion and inconsistency and humor. I remembered how sick she had been in China, and how she couldn't eat anything but cucumbers. I remembered how, at a gut level, Pat had understood things about China that the rest of us tended to intellectualize.

"And you know, Shirley," she said finally, "something Yeh said sticks in my mind. It was the last night we were there. She was tellin' me about workin' for the travel service for two years, and how when we left, she had been assigned to work in the fields for six months. I asked her what she'd really like to do, and she said, 'Be a teacher, a school teacher.' I asked her why she couldn't do that if she wanted to, and she said, 'Because my job is the job they picked out for me.' That sticks in my mind, because over here you have the right to be anything you want."

Among all of us, Margaret Whitman had been the most resilient. She had remained cheerful and energetic throughout the trip, revealing very little of the inner confusion she must have felt. The key to her self-control lay in her background. "To control oneself under any and all circumstances was how I was raised," she said.

"But now I think I'll cut loose and really swing. I've decided I never really was a conservative person. I just thought I should be because everyone around me was."

Margaret traveled alone around the world after she left China, but not before urging the rest of the delegation to take advantage of the same opportunity while they were still young. She wrote me a letter from Singapore, which I shall treasure always. She talked about how reluctant, even embarrassed, she had always been to express her deep feelings. "But my admiration for the Chinese and their feelings is so boundless that I'm going to change. I feel newly liberated," she wrote, "and my poor husband doesn't know whether to laugh or cry or both." He ended up loving the new Margaret.

Rosa Marin and Phyllis Kronhausen had cooler, more detached responses to China. They were professionals, schooled in social research, and had been educated to view things more objectively than the rest of us. That training tended to make their responses less personal. They found it difficult to personalize what they had seen, and seemed to cling to the notion that all truth was relative and had very little to do with them personally.

Throughout most of the journey, Rosa had remained separate from us, asking finally for a room by herself so she could study quietly at night. Because her translator had been Spanish-speaking, she perceived China in still another way. When she got home, she sat down and wrote articles about the experience. Enclosed in a letter sent from Israel, where she was doing still another field trip, she sent me the articles.

"If there's an elite in China," she wrote, "it's the

masses; and the masses are the workers, peasants, and soldiers. They carry the most weight and influence. According to our standards, perhaps, they are poor. But their poverty is equally divided. There's no chasm between rich and poor."

Her articles, filled with reportorial detail, dealt in general with the "helpfulness and honesty of the revolutionary society." But she also saw some of China's shortcomings. She didn't approve at all of the state choosing one's profession, even if the individuals involved were happy to comply. And she spoke several times of the artistic isolation (in China there are no foreign films or books or magazines or papers available to the general populace), and the lack of artistic individuality. "If an artist paints a picture, his name doesn't appear," she wrote. "Anonymity is stressed. Individuality is submerged." She thought that after Mao's death he would become a kind of Buddha figure, quoted and revered by everybody.

"But I think the Chinese understand that the real revolution is within the self," she wrote, "not with abstract platitudes, but with concrete action."

Phyllis was most impressed with the speed with which the Chinese "had achieved a complete turnabout in values and goals, and at a relatively low cost." She thought it was questionable, even sad, that the centuries-old Chinese artistic tradition had been altered or done away with, perhaps permanently. "The present system," she went on, "severely pressures all nonconformists, intellectuals, artists, and so on, but then *most* Chinese never had any identification with people like that anyway, since 95 per cent of China is peasant. So to the Chinese, that sacrifice doesn't mean much."

Phyllis agreed with the others that "what is so impressive about the Chinese is their happiness and warmth
with each other. They have a meager standard of living
compared to the West, but they are relating more to
the intercommunication between themselves than what
they want to own. The de-emphasis of the individual in
China is successful because it had to be. And it might be
the future of the entire world, including the United
States, unless we solve our overpopulation problem. Man
is a sociable animal who is interdependent; and inter-
dependence and individuality are extremely difficult attitudes to maintain when the pressure of numbers is great.
The more people there are, the more the tendency for
conservatism and de-emphasis of individuality."

In the hospital, Phyllis learned a great deal about still
another China, spending long hours talking with the
nurses and doctors. She seemed very much changed by
this experience.

"It was important for me to see with my own eyes
that China was working," she said. "I couldn't decipher
the propaganda from the truth until I saw it for myself.
I appreciate the experience more than I can say, because
it gave me faith that people can change. As a psychologist, I now feel that we psychologists have a purpose.
When I get discouraged these days, I think about what
the Chinese have done. I'm just sorry we aren't more
free to travel because we can all learn from each other.
One of the biggest mistakes China is making, by the
way, is that they are not learning that much from the
outside world. But I wish we were more free to learn
from them. The key to whether a society is alive and
happy is that it constantly strives to be better. That is
what the Chinese are up to."

When Karen Boutillier went to China she was bright
and articulate and twelve years old. I suppose that the experience is something that will mean more to her in the
future than it did at the time. In China, she frequently
seemed confused about her reactions, as if she were
expressing what she was *supposed* to feel, instead of
what she truly felt. She certainly must have been emotionally affected by the demoralization of the American
adults in the delegation. So, if Karen appeared to absorb
very little of China, it was probably because she found it
painful to be around us. When I talked to her on the
phone, she still hadn't fully begun to define the experience.

"My friends say I've changed when I talk to them,"
she said. "I ask them what they mean, and they say I act
different. They treat me special now. So I can never tell
whether they like me for me or for who I am because I'm
famous now. I tell them about the Great Wall and the
Forbidden City and the Children's Palace and meeting
Madame Chou En-lai. And then I tell them how the
Chinese are so warm with each other. Some of my
friends want to know if Mao Tse-tung is a king or a
god or something, and I tell them his words and sayings
are part of everyday life and that they praise him all the
time. Some asked me if that was all a show, and I said
no, I thought it was real. Some wondered if they only
showed us the good things and I said no, they seemed to
let us go anywhere we wanted except Mongolia. But they
sometimes wonder if *I'm* putting on a show."

"Are you?"

"Well, no," Karen said, with some hesitation. "But
there's something I wanted to ask you. You know, I'm

going on 'To Tell the Truth.' I wonder—how should I act?"

The four crew members—Claudia Weill, Cabell Glickler, Joan Weidman, and Nancy Shreiber—had been the most deeply shaken by the experience of China. They were there not as spectators but to work. That made the culture shock even more severe. As filmmakers they were required to interpret visually a society they couldn't understand easily or quickly. They had to work without viewing rushes (previous day's filming) and their anxieties were heightened by the pressure of limited time, inadequate planning, and equipment that sometimes broke down. The result was that each one of them, at one time or another, felt helpless, insecure, and incapable of handling the job. Since the four of them were highly intelligent, well-trained, and qualified women, these unavoidable circumstances offended their sense of professionalism. When they found themselves being observed by their Chinese sisters, the frustration was doubly painful.

In retrospect, I believe that the fundamental problem *all* of us were having in China had to do with the image we had of ourselves as women. What influenced us most in China, beyond economic progress, or food production, or the organized unity of the masses, or even how pleasant the Chinese were to each other, was how the *Chinese women* behaved with the *Chinese men*. There it was, on a primitive and fundamental level. *The ease of equality.* We saw it all around us every day. The Chinese women were dressed in nondescript, unisex clothes, with no make-up, no jewelry, no professional hair-styling.

They had none of the traditional feminine fripperies. Yet, precisely because they were not preoccupied with such things, they appeared secure in their femininity and there was a lovely ease in their relationships with men.

We saw arguments and disagreements between husbands and wives, or coworkers, male and female, or students, but sex was never a factor. There were no flirtatious glances or hostile putdowns woven into the arguments. The *subject* of the disagreement was more important than how the argument was conducted.

The Chinese women didn't seem to want to be "better" than men, or "as good as men." They were more interested in extending *themselves* to the limits of their own capacities. They were trying *their* best and usually were able to equal or surpass the men who worked beside them. If they didn't, they didn't seem irritated or dejected (especially on the communes where physical strength was a factor). Instead, they accepted circumstances matter-of-factly, somehow secure in the knowledge that there were other areas of life where they excelled. There was no evidence of the kind of sad power game that some of our women find themselves playing so often.

This realization was shattering for all of us, but especially for the crew. It was so easy to fall into the trap of competing with men instead of living up to one's own potential. It was tempting to treat the male as the enemy in the frustrating struggle for equality. This was an attitude totally incomprehensible to the Chinese women. When we discussed women's liberation with the Chinese women, they would ask about the militant feminists in America, whom the Chinese believed to be good soldiers and organizers. When we described how far some Western feminists had gone in rejecting men, the Chinese couldn't believe us. A battle of the sexes was beyond their comprehension and they didn't see the need for such extreme defense mechanisms. Certainly we saw no sexist attitudes in any circumstances while we were in China (which is not to say that they do not exist in subtle ways).

In addition to all the other value confusions, culture shock, and simple foreignness, I believe the insight into our sex roles in the West was what made us break down. The accidental presence of the satellite crew on the ninth floor of the Minzu Hotel didn't help matters any, because the Western men tended to re-emphasize and reinforce the male-female game playing that we, as a women's delegation, had begun to understand we needed to avoid.

Even though we felt alternately shaken and enlightened by our observations of the Chinese women, the crew members were the most affected, because they considered themselves feminists. All their basic notions of work, art, sex and sex roles, individualism, women's liberation, and child rearing were suddenly turned upside down. It was painful to admit that most of what we had mouthed about women's liberation in America was just words; what we saw in action in China so disturbed us that we got physically sick.

I've seen Claudia many times since returning, because we edited the film together. She did a magnificent job of filmmaking, and has learned to trust her craft and professionalism more as a result. From a personal point of view she said, "China has helped me to drop many of the façades I carried with me as a feminist. I feel more honest now, and I insist on more honesty with the people in my life."

Nancy wanted to go back to China immediately. Angered by the exclusionary policies of the electricians union in New York, which would not allow women members, she was constantly reminded of the example of China, where equality was a matter of official policy and was enforced. Nancy cut her hair short, lost weight, and found satisfaction in working on a film with a woman director. She said, "I have set aside the experience of China, somewhere in my mind where whenever I need calm and serenity I can touch it."

Cabell broke a bone in her back soon after returning to America, and spent some time in the hospital. She said the insensitivity of the American doctors and nurses were in brutal contrast to the gentleness she had seen in China. For the first time in her life she said she became enraged over the treatment of the poor in America and concluded that "once you see China, it's impossible ever again to view America as you always had."

Joan's experience with China had more to do with her own self-discipline than anything else. She was still angry with herself for behaving badly in the hospital in Canton. "I wanted to complete my job," she said. "I've never had any patience with either myself or unavoidable problems. I've always figured I can prevail through an act of will. China taught me to loosen up—not to be so rigid with myself—to relax with the inevitable when it's clear that that's what's happening. The Chinese won their revolution by having patience with themselves. I learned from them."

So our journey was over and now we were back home again leading our lives. The twelve of us became very close during those four weeks in China, even though we were strangers in the beginning. We got to know each other in ways that never would have happened in the United States, and formed a bond that would last the rest of our lives.

I spent some time with Margaret and Phyllis talking about our "time on the other planet." But, except for the calls I placed to them, and my work on the film with Claudia, I never heard from the others again.

As for me, across the months, I began to understand how the astronauts must have felt after coming back from the moon. At dinner parties, people asked questions and I tried my best to answer, but they usually responded with "and then what?". The experience was still too raw, too unformed, too difficult to explain with words. Like the moon, you had to have been there.

But that clearly wasn't good enough. I'd spent all my adult life communicating with people, in one way or another. I should then be able to communicate the essence of China. But as the months moved on, I realized how inadequate words could be when it came to defining a very large idea. People asked if I could live there. I told them no, I couldn't live in China; it was not my country, I didn't understand the language, I couldn't handle the restrictions China would place on my personality. But I suspected that if I could live there, I would be a better human being. Again, I couldn't explain *why* with any precision; but I knew that I wouldn't be as concerned with myself, my needs, my possessions, my desires. In China, I would learn to be less selfish, more concerned with others, more sensitive to those around me. And the reason was simple. I would be taught—or re-educated, as would be the case for people of my generation—*not* to think so exclusively about myself. The society itself would continually remind me to think of the existence of others. In other words—and the first time I realized it I shuddered—I would be "conditioned."

I thought a lot about that.

In a completely different way, of course, I had been conditioned in the West since birth. The conditioning happened in the schools I attended, in the streets of Virginia after school, in New York when I was a young dancer, in the pages of newspapers and magazines, and through movies and television. There were many values transmitted to me during that conditioning process: fear of communism, a belief in the "American way" (which meant, of course, a belief in capitalism). There were cynical values too: "Everybody has a price"; "Politicians are crooks"; "More money means more happiness." And all the values revolved around the individual self. As a kid, I heard grown-ups mouth the slogan "Take care of number one," as if self-concern and Americanism were synonymous. As an adult American, I watched American bombs obliterate Asian villages. Was that so that America itself could be Number One? In some ways, America had grown up to be a masterpiece of self concern.

I was an individualist, convinced that freedom meant *personal* freedom; the inalienable right to do anything you wanted, so long as it did not hurt others. And then suddenly I was in China, where individualism did not exist. And I was extraordinarily happy. I stopped smoking the second day I was there. I stopped a lifelong nervous habit of picking my fingers and biting my nails. I began enjoying sunsets and trees and food instead of rushing through each day because time meant money. There didn't seem to be enough hours in the day to enjoy life, and I slept less because I felt so much more alive when I was awake.

I sighed less, even though there were days when I felt dragged down by the obligations of making the film and keeping the delegation together. But those were details. What was important was that every day I felt powerful vibrations because of the massive, anonymous, healthy group of human beings called the Chinese people. It was a sense that superseded language, that seemed to have little to do with economics or philosophy, and everything to do with shared humanity. China was a communal society, and yet it seemed to have created a sense of individual harmony, where all of its parts were integrated with the whole.

And so I began to wonder whether a communal style of life wasn't what nature intended in the first place. Perhaps "communalism" was another way of describing harmony. Certainly contact with an apparently harmonious society was what touched all of us in China. Perhaps Western values, for the past five hundred years, had been a human distortion, perhaps competition was simply not compatible with harmony, not conducive to human happiness, perhaps the competitive urge came only from the exaggerated emphasis on the individual. Maybe the individual was simply not as important as the group.

When I put these pieces of the Chinese puzzle together I had to question what "the American way of life"—my own way—really meant in view of what I had seen in China. According to the American ethic, free competition on all levels was necessary for progress and initiative. We had been taught to be ready to die for that freedom, rather than face the possibility of "their way of life." Now I was questioning what all of that meant. Was it possible for a society to be viable if it concerned itself more with what it could *give* rather than what it could *get?* And was that concept too frightening, too diametrically opposed to our way of thinking to be considered practical? Was that why China was so basically threatening to us?

I suppose what shook me the most about China was that it completely altered my notions about human nature. I used to believe human nature was absolute; it had been a foregone conclusion to me that certain flaws and weaknesses were basic and permanent. If faced with the existence of evil, I would shrug and say, "Well, that's human nature." If someone stole, cheated, murdered, or was outrageously greedy, I would often dismiss the behavior as par for the course. I had plenty of evidence for the proposition that man was basically selfish, aggressive, fearful, savage, and greedy.

But I couldn't feel that way anymore. I had seen an entire nation, once degraded, corrupt, demoralized, and exploited, that was changing its very nature. In changing the political, economic, and material nature, they had caused the better side of human nature to dominate. Certainly in a country of 800,000,000 people there are those who are still selfish, cruel, evil, and greedy. But the vast majority are full of group pride, full of kindness and decency to each other, peace-loving and humane.

I realized that if what we call human nature can be changed, then absolutely *anything* is possible. And from that moment, my life changed.

There was a final paradox: After contact with a society that was communal, that smothered its creative culture, and saw art only as a way of serving the revolution, I began again to think about being an artist.

The intricacies of American politics suddenly bored me, and I no longer felt the need to travel to faraway places. I had my talent to think about now. I had spent too much time denying that talent, abusing it through misuse, being casual with it, or running from it. I had never really learned its limits. I had never really taken the talent I had on a long march.

After China I realized that the talent was there to be refurbished, to be nurtured, to be stretched to its furthest limits and made into something that would not only "serve the people" of my own country, but also serve myself. I was not a soldier or a philosopher or a politician; I could cure no disease, solve no economic problems, or lead any revolutions. But, I could dance. I could sing. I could make people laugh. I could make people cry.

A week later, I walked into a dance studio for the first time in twenty years.

A year later, I opened in Las Vegas. There were cheers and reporters and flashbulbs and celebrities, and a lone waiter who stood in a corner with tears rolling down his face and hands reaching out to touch me from the darkness. At the end, as the house lights came up, I saw a fourteen-year-old girl sitting with her family and I

wanted to tell her about life and about nature and about
harmony. I wanted to tell her to cherish her life, her
country, the earth she was part of. I wanted to tell her
to love it all back, to fight despair and hatred and greed
with every muscle in her body. I wanted to tell her about
China, and about all the glorious possibilities of life if
you believe hard enough. "You can't get there from
here" the cliché went. But you could. I was getting
there.

In the dressing room a reporter made his way through
the crush and asked me why I had come back again to
the live stage. I talked about the need to see people's
faces and hear their laughter and make contact with as
many as possible. And then I heard myself say, "Actually,
Mao Tse-tung is probably responsible for my being here."
The reporter looked puzzled. He laughed nervously and
asked me what I meant. Margaret Whitman, jovial and
ever cheerful, was standing amidst the flowers and telegrams in the crowded room. "Ask her," I said. He did.
And Margaret said, "Yes, that's right. China makes you
believe that everything is possible."

The day was about to break when I finally left the
hotel to go home. Great mauve smears rose over the
desert mountains. I stood for a moment and listened to
the wind as it moved from the mountains, pushing weeds
and sand before it. A program from my show rattled in
the parking lot.

I suddenly felt that the wind was the same wind that
blew in China, blowing across oceans, valleys, and mountain ranges, all the way across the world to Nevada. To
me it was a wind of possibility, a wind of hope. Not a
Chinese wind, really, nor an American wind for that

matter. But a wind made of the air that belonged to all of us.

I walked to the car and got in and drove home through the deserted, windy streets. Somewhere around the third traffic light, I realized I was singing.